FALLEN CHURCHES

Evil Influence of Liberalism Across the Board

KAREN KELLOCK PH.D.

Manual for
Superior Men

A complete theory based on Einstein physics, Political Psychology, Systems Theory and Archetypal Psychiatry.

FORMULA

All success attraction
All disease obstruction
All recovery elimination

You must fast on all three
OBSTRUCTIONS:
People
Habit
Food

FALLEN CHURCHES

The Latter Days is the era of preachers from hell and the churches are SOCIAL. It's a curse: evil is spreading fast in false doctrines that degrade the church. For when men cease to believe in God they do not believe in nothing but are capable of believing anything. When no one knows what true character is they fall to evil devices. Churches are full of new age leaven and much of it's due to the paganism of ruling women. Licentiousness is the new morality of the secular system who wants homeschool illegal. It has all imploded together: fallen churches and dysfunctional families, a catastrophe.

FALLEN CHURCHES

Evil Influence of Liberalism Across the Board

FALLEN CHURCHES

Evil Influence of Liberalism Across the Board

IT'S LIKE A CLUB
VACCINES FROM DISEASED ANIMALS
SOCIETY'S FALSENESS AND FEMINISM
AGEISM IS WORSE THAN RACISM
FEMALE TYRANTS
SWEET LITTLE LADIES UNITE!
WHAT CAME FIRST?
JEZEBEL MAL-ADAPTATIONS
WOLVES DRESSED AS LAMBS
PEOPLE PROBLEMS VS WORKING ON SELF
WITNESSING THE DARK SIDE
IT WAS HORRIBLE LIVING WITH LIBERALS
STOP WASTING TIME
DON'T GO TO THEIR PAGES!
INDEPENDENCE IS ANATHAMA
DON'T EVER GO WITH EM
BE NICE IS CULTURAL DECLINE
BY GETTING ENTANGLED
HANDLING DISRESPECT
WHAT THEY PUT ME THROUGH
PH.D. IN THE STREETS
FRIENDLESS CAN BE BLISS
APPROVAL-GETTING
HE'S NOT THAT INTO YOU

FALLEN CHURCHES

Evil Influence of Liberalism Across the Board

FALLEN CHURCHES

Evil Influence of Liberalism Across the Board

DRAMA IS TOO COSTLY
LIFE IS A PIE: DON'T WASTE ENERGY
FORGIVE PEOPLE, LOVE ELEMENTS
EXHAUSTION FROM CODEPENDENCY
WITLESS WOMEN
EVIL IS AN ENDLESS RABBIT HOLE
LOVE ADDICTION
CALUMNY IS SOUL MURDER
DON'T LET EM HURT YOU TWICE
EMOTIONALLY BLOCKED FROM EARLY TRAUMA
ARTISTICALLY EXPRESSING HURT
WORSHIP IS FORTIFICATION
THE CHILD NEEDS YOUR ATTENTION
CURE: CREATE A SPACE FOR SELF
HELLO, GOODBYE
HURT TWICE, NO DICE
FOR HEALTH REASONS
KAREN'S HEALTHY CANDIES
FORGET NIGHTSHADES, THINK STORAGE
FOOD STORAGE FOR THIS THEORY
LONG HAIR
CORONAVIRUS AND 5G
WITHOUT GOD THE SYSTEM IS A DRUG
HOW TO BE A DIVINE WRITER

FALLEN CHURCHES

Evil Influence of Liberalism Across the Board

It all imploded together: fallen churches and dysfunctional families--thus begun this tragedy.

The churches should have saved us from all this but since they've been fallen it's a wide open ditch.

NEW AGE AND GOSPEL DISTORTION

Evil is spreading fast as shown in false doctrines and preachers degrading the church: it's a curse.

When men cease to believe in God they do not believe in nothing, but are capable of believing anything.

The rejection of the moral order of the created universe results in radical evil--Germany's legalizing it all.

Germany: licentiousness is the new morality of the secular materialist establishment and homeschool is illegal.

The simple gospel of salvation: We are saved from sin, death and hell not by works but Christ ALONE.

Salvation is APART from any works, ceremonies or ordinances! Those are phony, flashy falsehoods.

Salvation results in a transformed life which PRODUCES righteous works--but no works contribute to it.

FALLEN CHURCHES

We're then justified by God, the Holy Spirit is given and transformation is seen in every aspect of livin'.

First churches were converted outa paganism and redeemed but then false teachers showed up.

These false teachers were Satan disguised as ministers of light. They're all over the place, you know the type.

They didn't have an anti-Christian message but a DEVIANT quasi-Christian message which is most deceptive.

They said they believed in Jesus Christ but they ALSO said "that's not sufficient to save you"--that's the crux.

They added the RULES, ordinances, ceremonies and rituals of the Law of Moses--old boring stuff.

It said they couldn't go from paganism to the Kingdom of God--they had to go thru the rules of Judaism.

PAUL SHOCKED BY DISTORTIONS

Paul was shocked at the distortions and called it a "different gospel"--giving no relief from hell.

People were deserting Him who called em--God Himself--and the Good News Gospel for Bad News from Hell.

The danger is a distorted message not an anti-Christian one: Salvation is from faith PLUS works: no fun.

Paul said anyone preaching a different gospel need be cursed, damned, an anathema.

You preach another gospel you'll be cursed and damned by God himself--it's faith ALONE Paul said.

There is NO worse position for a person to be in than to be a false teacher propagating lies: the biggest sin.

FALLEN CHURCHES

False teachers twist scripture to pervert the true gospel which then clouds the ONLY way of salvation.

False doctrine leads one down the wrong path making Christ useless while being obligated to the law.

False doctrine is damning--no grace, a total waste--and thus they are "damnable heresies" Paul says.

What is grace for? FREEDOM--that's why Christ sets us free. Not a "works system": a yoke of slavery.

It's the freedom not to sin but to do what is RIGHT. Not a buncha laws that we can't possibly keep.

The false teachers acknowledged Christ but added WORKS to the faith and that's the blasphemy.

The false teachers acknowledged Christ but added WORKS to the faith and that's the blasphemy.

The false doctrine of FAITH + WORKS comprises most of the Christians in the world--a MASSIVE error.

INFINITE FALSEHOODS

False forms of Christianity abound. They believe in the "true God" but then add WORKS, wrecking it all.

False teachers hinder us from the truth. Posing as scholars they put up obstacles/nothing's smooth.

False teachers immediately turn their back on faith and walk right into legalism and destruction.

False teachers are ungodly and do not obey the truth-- faith alone in Christ alone--but say we gotta "do".

Saying we gotta "DO" brings God's wrath/indignation--for it's a brick to carry not a lamp to guide, and it's boring.

FALLEN CHURCHES

Why would these false teachers compel you to works? To make a good SHOWING in the flesh, period.

They believed in the CROSS of Christ but didn't abandon their judaistic practices in fear of persecution.

They were making a good showing in the flesh in ADDITION to saying they believed in the cross.

Yah, they wanted to hold on to all of this for their own personal, business and social BENEFITS.

Severed from grace, they'd never attain the righteousness they pursue cuz that's only in Christ not the pew.

False teachers infiltrate--they introduce destructive heresies like "we're all one" then it's bad fate.

They introduce new words and God has set them for judgement. They're all around and a curse, amen.

IT'S SATAN'S CHURCH

It's Satan's church even though Christianity is it's label. Wolves in sheep's clothing--you're disabled.

These legalistic lies--that you gotta do this and that--are not from God but the purveyors God despises.

The naive think: "but they must have SOME connection to God" but they do not--they are the OPPOSITE.

False teachers contaminate the church. A little leaven is that permeating evil influence/doesn't take much.

The evil permeating influence is always sin and false doctrine. When I joined a church I lost freedom.

The greatest leaven were the Pharisees, the most fastidious legalistic jews of outward appearances.

FALLEN CHURCHES

Paul said the teaching of false doctrine "EATS" like gangrene. They were mean, I escaped the scene.

The Pharisees were the symbol of this invisible permeating corruption. They get inside, they feast on it.

They love being seen in occasions giving them credibility. They insist you go, tho' it's all boring and silly.

They wanted acceptance. Paul would have been had he held on to the trappings of Judaism + the cross.

False teachers always persecute true teachers if they tell the truth [and not waiver or give in to slander].

It's not easy to say that's all there is--that it's faith + **NOTHING**--and to hell with made up things.

The cross settles it ALL--you don't have to do **ONE THING** even go to church, especially now they've fallen.

MESSAGE: CHRIST ONLY [PAUL]

The message of the cross--Christ and Him crucified--was the only message Paul ever preached.

Paul called any **SLIGHT** deviation from the gospel as full-fledged pagans who may as well be castrated!

Aberrant Christianity is no different from a pagan religion--and this includes most of the church body today.

Religion should be the bridge to the divine, but is usurped by Satan's workers calling themselves "preachers".

Preachers: There is **NO** room for any alteration of gospel of faith for salvation and **ALL WORKS** are death.

Gospel: We're saved by Christ alone apart from any works, ordinances, ceremonies or **CHURCH ATTENDANCE.**

FALLEN CHURCHES

Galatians is a book of polemics between Paul defending the true gospel and interlopers/false teachers.

There's always religion since man is made for God. He has a natural thirst for the divine outside of himself.

Why are there so many FORMS of religion? Satan. He confuses things and deliberately is falsifyin'

RECAP on modern preachers: Those who see themselves as God's representatives are full-fledged pagans.

Satan knows all truths about God, the crucifixion and the trinity. But as arch-hater of God he denies all three.

Works churches are mental slavery. They are bricks to carry not lamps to guide, bringing misery.

Mormons were angry I wanted to stay home/work all the time, I was supposed to go to boring meetings.

NOTHING HAPPENING IN THEIR MEETINGS

Nothing happening in their meetings and staying home was replete with meaning so I escaped the scene.

That's totally why people turn against Christianity--because of false churches blocking eternity.

Same with prayer meetings: boring, social and late as they wait for stragglers. No self-discipline I wager.

I asked myself early: "this seems like pure paganism and collectivism, this can't be God--or can it really?"

Why so many religions? The answer is simple: there is only ONE God and millions of demons.

So there is one true church and the rest of them Satan in the multiplicity of his forms.

FALLEN CHURCHES

Satan knows there's only One Way to heaven so he has proliferated as many religions as he can.

The earth is overrun with all kinds of forms of false religion from demons and the evil hearts of men.

Either salvation is solely by God thru divine accomplishment [the cross] or by man, thru human achievement.

True religion relieves man's sin--it's reconciling. False religion is just various ways to cover that shame.

God performs miracles often through a woman. In that case she must have an understanding husband.

True religion is always slaughtered by false religion which leads to massacre against the people of God.

FALLEN CHURCHES = DYSFUNCTIONAL FAMILIES

It all imploded together: fallen churches and dysfunctional families--thus begun this tragedy.

If you give woman an edge to be evil she may be evil and not think of the damage to other people.

The boys taking over small towns as the cops stand down are now transients in big cities--the violent ones.

I was scared then and ever since in PTSD symptoms. Violent youth will do anything, I fear em.

I will **NOT** be on the begging end with you. After going thru all this I just want a good man/reliable too.

Just by asserting myself, my boundaries or convictions would bring violence from the young dumbed.

I'm in a new life now, away from danger. But the PTSD memories are lucid like as if I'm right there.

FALLEN CHURCHES

The youth are insane and dangerous. All over the world it's the YOUNG men who are rapacious/violent.

All ethics and morals have been stripped away so there's no predicting what they'll do not getting their way.

All they see is easy carefree MURDER in video games and movies and when frustrated merely copy it sir.

COMMUNIST SPIRIT IN THE YOUTH

The communist spirit has so taken over they just take what they want whether maid or housekeeper.

Just by disciplining or drawing boundaries mom suddenly finds her pet missing: it's common Missy.

They can't stand correction one bit. They'll get you back, probably by proxy as your world goes black.

The small town had enough of this young thug so now he's a big city transient, stealin' and dealin'.

Wouldn't report attempted rape outa fear for her dogs so cops did a sting and he was years locked up.

After going thru this I don't tolerate mind games of any kind. Life's too short to fall into these grinds.

Aggressive, nasty youth with hippie, loser, beta or feminist parents and nothing but liberal brainwashed.

Liberals are the cult of absolute selfishness and getting what you want backed up with violence.

Demons turned loose on the earth came right to my home doing Satan's work to obstruct, steal, kill, curse.

Up to that time I was trusting, naive, submissive to crime. Now my whole thing is isolation/drawing lines.

FALLEN CHURCHES

These are frightening days and now they say we won't even be able to breath with lungs ablaze.

Help us Lord, the churches have fallen and there's no one helpin' and all the respirators are gone.

It's soon the law of the jungle dealing with the lowest animals who will kill you for bare essentials.

Steve Jobs the creator of Apple wouldn't give his kids an Ipad cuz it "brain damages" em/makes em sad.

5G doesn't cause coronavirus, it pushes it into the cells.

Was she grinding a stick up your nose as a test OR implanting microchips? Think about that.

The virus test is unnecessarily painful. Putting a stick up your nose and grinding it into the flesh? Awful

And having it done by some petty cog in the wheel who wants to show power? It's serious lover.

I gotta write what comes up and I rarely question it. Only later do I see why I did it.

THE OLD CHURCH KEPT US STABLE

Vibrant churches of old kept things stable, at least as a symbol but now the crosses are gone/illegal.

When this happens we lose our hedge of protection and evil flows in unobstructed: laws of the fallen.

WE determine our protection: it's a given if repentant and on the right side of God, our Champion.

When in sin I had no protection from evil which flowed in. When repentant the hedge was back, safe again.

FALLEN CHURCHES

Is it possible God our Father is using PANIC to wake us up? Life as we knew it is over--good luck.

So you had the devil inside ya', directing every action. This is nothing new, it's humans since time began.

The narc doesn't do the abuse, he facilitates it thru a third party or even a group so he stays clean too.

The narc abuse can be ostracizing you or making you feel inferior thru others down-putting your worth.

It's always about power and control: how can I put her down? Getting her outa her house is the goal.

False religion is damning deception and Satan's disguised as an angel of light operating with his ministers.

The warning against false religion is also the "doctrines of demons" into which the masses are drawn.

The best lie is the one with the most truth in it. New World Order Game Plan

This is serious. We're either on the brink of depression or jubilee with all debts, mortgages written off free.

EVIL GOSSIP OF FLYING MONKEYS

A subtle flying monkey tactic of the narcissist is to bring evil gossip--what they "said about you".

Or "they don't know why I like you, they say you're poor". Evil messengers are not your friends, ignore.

Lesson ONE: STAY AWAY from flying monkeys, abuse by proxy and their cajolers after you said "NO".

Flying monkeys are ENFORCERS who will drain your soul of worth and self-esteem cuz they are mean.

FALLEN CHURCHES

You need every bit of the self-esteem you can get for your own evolution--it's drained away by group thugs.

If you say **NO** to someone and next comes his friend to cajole you to say **YES**, that's a monkey fortress.

Since we no longer have true doctrine or sense of God, we fall into these traps of humans, the flawed.

It used to be if a woman was harassed by frenemies a church brother would take care of it, see?

PASTORS PLAYED PROTECTIVE DADDY

I told pastor and he'd go the boys house to tell em to **NEVER, EVER** bother me again, just as promised.

I told pastor about the Jezebel army/her dangerous jealousies and he'd remove her from my life, see?

Pastor was the angry protective father I never had. He wasn't weak but **BOLD** as saints were instructed.

Humans will **TRAP** you and tho' you never made a commitment will **KILL** you if you resist them.

The answer is: don't get involved! Always keep your home as your power base, stay with your own.

WEAKNESS AND REPETITION COMPULSION

You must work on yourself [personal development] to stop repetition compulsion: going after dingbats.

We're on the Freudian system of **REPEAT** if we never got our needs met early, see? So we like Mary/Steve.

Infancy is the only time needs are externally met, later we can only meet em ourselves, not thru Mary/Jack.

FALLEN CHURCHES

Twenty years total social isolation in the desert wilderness built an inner identity/reality for me, yes sir.

When we can't let go of someone it means he's not good for us. Not some angel tho' that's the gloss.

You're not hanging on to a man/woman but something you never got. You got em on a pedestal for naught.

It's something you needed as a desperate rejected infant and that's why you can't let go I think.

FALLEN CHURCHES/INFERIOR PERSONALITIES

Once the churches were fallen all these complications from inferior personalities started happening.

Healthy neuropathway in your brain says this guy loves you/is no good for you--but it can be reversed too.

From a desperate clinger to stinkers to a self-reliant person firmly grounded in one's OWN reality.

If you were imprinted towards rejection then you'll always be like a baby duck swimming upstream, drownin'

Instead of being a duck following it's mother you're a joker following the rejector cuz you're a REPEATER.

As neuropathways are being rebuilt as to what things mean you'll be uncomfortable with nice guys, see?

BROKEN EARLY BONDS AND CADS

You're not holding onto Jack/Julie but projections of unmet needs from childhood, a dull ache.

It was terrifyingly delicious and addicting, this dull ache I was projecting onto others who didn't like me.

FALLEN CHURCHES

A dull ache always seeking correction and never completing, one that made me very needy.

Someone opened up a can of worms in me cuz it blended with emotion as deep as the ocean, and words.

You can't get over someone if you're idolizing them. You've gotta see em for who they are ma'am.

We cannot get faith in our unregenerated nature. We RECEIVE faith, a new voice: whole, mature.

It's no problem social distancing. I've always broken the chain/flattened the curve, it's my thing.

GOD SAVES WHILE STILL IN SIN

God saved me while I was still in sin. I can't get over that--what extreme grace, though I didn't know it then.

He just wanted me to LEARN from what I was enduring but He also saved me after sufficient hurting.

It is strange to have PTSD about events half my life ago yet other eras fade below or were slow.

It was just like it was yesterday, these noxious events that so imprinted they are re-experienced constantly.

The nerve of that guy imposing on me like that--yet meaningless today, it was just an archetype.

Churches of old emphasized CHARACTER but now they do NOT since sins are accepted along with other rot.

When character is gone there are no friends and a jungle mentality takes over, there is no trust man.

In the old days church members were mindful of every tiny cue of bad character, now it's a bother.

FALLEN CHURCHES

FALLEN CHURCHES AND CODEPENDENCY;

When the churches fell we stopped seeing ourselves as children of God--with men we were awed.

Codependent becomes obsessed with narcissist because she can't understand the confusion he creates.

Obsession with confusion ENDS when no-contact begins. Mark off your calendar for each day of silence.

NO CONTACT is so important for the codependent it must be stringent, adamant, absolute, life or death.

The more noncommittal he is the more obsessed she becomes. Stop this bagashit: GROW UP/reject bums.

You need your self-love badly. Be like the First Lady: avoid totally the loveless, apathetic, shady.

To those thinking they can hang on or convince them not to treat you badly: you can't, hear me?

SEE YOURSELF AS THE FLOTUS

See yourself as if you are the FLOTUS. Would she allow that silly narcissist to treat her like this?

At the first sign of narcissist ghosting, fade-out or disrespect you need to be gone not in "love".

At the first sign of the shady you need to walk away--gently but suddenly--thanking heavenly Daddy.

Think back: What were those clear signs you ignored? His language, views, past-times in pop culture.

You knew it all along but infantile urges to correct early rejection took over with passionate surges.

FALLEN CHURCHES

A mind can be destroyed for years from one's betrayal, backstabbing, gossiping, triggered fears.

Go no-contact then pray for a solution. Once cleared of that dragon in comes a dashing panacea, oh man.

You break the no-contact and you go back into hell with Jack and you gotta start all over again, heck.

God doesn't want you with him any more than He'd want you on heroin—addiction to bad is the reason.

Stick to your true friends/youtube mentors and never, ever go there again. EVER, it's not an option man.

Your new pain-free life can start TODAY, right this minute. You'll never have to feel this way again [bitten].

I know you're curious but you cannot GO THERE. This is your test and God wants you to pass it dear.

LET IT GO. You've had many situations in life that are now forgotten or resolved—it's about GROWTH.

LOVE THOSE WHO HAVE GODLY LOVE

You couldn't change mommy or daddy so now as an adult you hang on to rejectors treating you so crappy.

It's a lot to get ahold of so to simplify just put a picture of FLOTUS up: attract only to those who LOVE.

Love only those who love you as God does. If you didn't have a father, substitute/focus on God's love.

If sad or unsatisfied, compare this stiff-necked creep with Jesus who loved you so much He died.

Psychological damage is as bad as physical and usually much worse as we can never forget the louse.

FALLEN CHURCHES

This is your test: Can you get beyond the pest? Meanwhile, question all attractions in the past.

Turn down the shiny object of temptation and God'll bring in a new direction of happy lovingness/home.

LOVE ADDICTIONS IN ADULTEROUS GENERATIONS

In adulterous generations, addictions to love/people are the most obdurate of all aberrations.

Keep comparing the creep to Dad or God. Never forget his past actions that were salacious or odd.

You were a kind and good person and they decided to DESTROY you from selfishness--it happens.

As she decided to move on she got two kittens to love on. Moving on: no more the narcissist's pawn.

If he ever made you feel bad you must see him as an unempathic cad and that's THAT.

NOTICE how you already feel better having started the no-contact plan. That's your sign man.

To get rid of godless users/confusers, take note and be grateful for all God has given thru the years.

When I finally went no-contact and meant it, the whole universe lit up--dear Lord, I was so elated!

By the mere decision to go no-contact I heard crows in the morning, crickets at night: I was back.

The whole world lit up and God was smiling at me! I rid the brute who made me a sad sack, I was free.

There had to be a problem or you wouldn't be so sad. By your mere decision you are FREE God said.

FALLEN CHURCHES

DEMONRATS

Left has turned movies into Satan-worshipping filth films of demonic imagery putting down Christians.

Democrats are lower than rats because they're not human, they're demons. Mike Adams

They're lower than rats because they kill their own children then celebrate it. Even rats don't do that.

Even rats protect their own children. So calling them demon-rats is an insult to rats. Mike Adams

Abortion up to birth [and after]: Don't call democrats human--they're subhuman filth below any animal.

Even the dumbest creatures you can imagine know the difference between male and female son.

Following empty dogma and slogans, the democrats are incredibly delusional and frankly, retarded.

Who kills their own children? Demons do: this infanticide has happened throughout history too.

The demonrats hate churches, Christianity, homeschooling and the idea of God nauseates them.

Just like all demons, the idea of Jesus Christ being involved in our world is repulsive to them.

They hate the word "Jesus" even more than they hate the word "family" which triggers them totally.

Who would've ever imagined that the word "green" would mean communism and death? See it/reject it.

Dems wanna remove "so help me God" from the oath of office--just like any demon like the rat Obama.

FALLEN CHURCHES

Can you believe the word GOD is so offensive? Not when you see them as demons--that's their consensus.

The word "God" causes neurological pain to creatures of Satan since they're the opposite of love, light, truth.

PAIN, HATE AND DECEPTION

Pain, hate and deception is the opposite of love, light and truth. Perhaps this explains your friends/family too.

The dems wanna block out the sun. It's called "dimming" cuz they hate the light and love sinning.

The sun is the source of warmth, heat, light and life. The sun is offensive to democrats so they fight it.

Global Dimming releases pollution into the stratosphere causing a plummeting of oxygen, so we smother.

The climate change mob wants to suffocate us through geoengineering/altering the earth's atmosphere.

Why are they doing this? It's their marching orders from Satan: to destroy God's earth, so they do it.

Since they're a contradiction they call themselves "earth savers": see chemtrails, city poopers, open borders.

Our democrat saviors: kill our babies, poison our food, open borders for invasion from antithetic cultures.

Dam Dems: Inject em with toxic medicine--at gun point--then block out their sunlight and suffocate them.

Then they lie to em in a toxic media campaign, make everyone hate em re: "global warming".

THEY'RE SAVING THE EARTH

FALLEN CHURCHES

Just like any serpent would say, they're "saving the earth" while destroying it. Wake up, study, get hep.

Stop saying you're "saving the earth" Greta--you are not, you're destroying it everywhere and in America.

They're medical vampires of children. They take their blood, the longevity treatment called "ambrosia"

Children's blood for longevity is 8 grand per liter and you can get it in San Francisco, the liberal poop city.

Baby killers like pizzagate drink their blood for longevity--we know this already, "ambrosia" is their legal remedy.

Global elite have been doing this for hundreds of years. Kidnapping, raping, vampiring and bloodletting.

RITUALISTIC CHILD ABUSE AND DEMS

It's ritualistic child abuse, trafficking and sacrifice. And to such things the evil dems turn a blind eye.

Those who hate God, goodness, family and church feed off the blood of children--that's always how it's been.

Some of these creepy dems are big campaign contributors to monsters like Hillary Clinton--they give millions.

Like all demons they erect Satanic while demolishing Christian monuments. They remove crosses.

They don't want our great leaders monuments--they wanna see Satan in the city parks and halls.

They wanna see the horns of half human/half beast statues. You've seen em: it's Satan.

Everything in media/movies has been dominated by weird Satanic imagery-- Hollywood is worshipping it, see.

FALLEN CHURCHES

It's inbred psychotic control freaks who bioengineer our lives/deaths, called "guardians of the earth".

The eugenics cult gives scientists money and power and then they are compromised. That's why.

IT'S LIKE A CLUB

It's like a club that you get higher up in by doing worse and worse stuff. Then they got you, sure enough.

You join up with the wrong people and it gets worse, inching up gradually. That's the elites, truly.

The most popular pop music stars have a "Satan" video. They celebrate demonic characters ya' know.

The Superbowl over the last few years has been dominated by demonic imagery: Satanists run the industry.

Hollywood, the music/TV industry, scriptwriters, Netflix all attack Christians and prop up demons.

God is truth/light but democrats are serpents: they are deceivers--they gain power then reverse promises.

Dems love us so much you can't protect yourself from violent illegal immigrants with sanctuary status.

We must protect the precious little migrant babies but when it comes to American children: KILL EM!

American babies are worthless to the left but migrant babies are precious and deserve legal status.

Vaccine tyranny is an assault on human beings tho' they COULD be made safe without aluminum/mercury.

Dems want vaccines to damage children, growing up without functioning neurology: success, hurray.

A brain-damaged autistic child who can't even dress or defend himself: that's their accomplishment.

Demonrats get one point for killing babies but more for making em suffer all their lives in autistic PAIN.

The vaccine industry is an extension of Satanism. Fill em with toxic chemicals wrecking their immune system.

VACCINES FROM DISEASED ANIMALS

Vaccines are made from diseased animals in a festering cocktail of toxic DNA/RNA injected into newborns.

Vaccines are medical cannibalism too, since they grind aborted babies into the mix, called "fetal tissue".

Vaccines are ritualistic child sacrifice. Would this be done by Christians who love God/children and hate lies?

It's done by demonic dark spirits serving Satan--so divide from family members who say they love em.

Grind up dead children, inject em into other children then feed off their pain and suffering: that's vaccination.

Demonrats are beyond sick--they're evil at every level and if you don't face it I'm gonna have to leave you.

Final proof of demon-infestation in liberals: They attack the only two Christian nations--America and Israel.

The TWO nations founded by Christianity are relentlessly assaulted for "white bigoted hateful patriarchy".

Demonrats are preparing planet Earth to turn it into hell and they're succeeding. Lord, come speedily.

Anderson Cooper isn't given 12 million a year to read the news but to read what he's told by global pukes.

FALLEN CHURCHES

Always a double standard: Chinese kill you at checkpoints but we can't stop em from coming here.

SOCIETY'S FALSENESS AND FEMINISM

No female genius can trust women friends--it's all about conformity, accepting the narrative, hating men.

When you see how weakened men are it is sad. Most homeless are men/they die in wars good or bad.

When she divorces him he falls outa structure and feels lost. Many commit suicide tho' they were boss.

The feminist-influenced wife wants to pick a bone on every point, gets angry at stupid stuff, is always outa joint.

She has to **MAKE HIM LISTEN** and man does this get tiring. Stupid stuff, false narratives, ignorant rants.

If you've ever argued with a feminist it soon becomes a yelling match--she interrupts and talks too much.

The fights become an ego thing where she **MUST** win--even if it means having him declared incompetent.

If his righteous indignation at bitching is seen as violence, she'll get him on mandatory drugs, a wipeout.

If she weakens in arguments with conservative husband, she'll re-arm on the horn with the other women.

She's always encouraged to fight back more until he **TOTALLY** surrenders by her feminist sisters.

After the fight is over it's those officious friends of hers he wants to sever-- now it's war they **ALL** declare.

Women initiate divorce 70% of the time--it's **ALWAYS** encouraged or initiated by her friends not worth a dime.

FALLEN CHURCHES

Transgenderism has always been around: bible speaks of evil cults of gender dysphoria: welcome to the past.

Hubby calls em butt buddies.

AGEISM IS WORSE THAN RACISM

Just as it's rude to push race in their face it's rude to push em in the mud due to their age--get that, ok?

Spin 'n image of her dad, chip off the old block, a throwback to great orators/scholars way back.

I see now mom was always right she just didn't always have the best way to express it, so what?

Seeing past actors as archetypes removes energy from memory as in our state we attracted the hillbilly.

Our lower archetype attracted their lower archetype but who you are today would never stand for it.

You were caricatured in your lower state. That's always how it is while the true self is distinct/good fate.

Handsome highschooler voted most likely to succeed: 30 years later he resembled a puffy cartoon character.

The lower archetypes are caricatured, the higher archetypes are unique, distinct and godly for sure.

FEMALE TYRANTS

The woman having tyranny over me wasn't ruled by logic but by feminist narrative/bully revenge, see?

I knew I'd had it when she was assigned. For an unspecified duration I was gonna lose my mind.

If you don't conform to a female tyrant she gets vindictive and mean which she calls tough but needed.

FALLEN CHURCHES

It's up to her what is "tough love" that's so needed, her excuse for the vindictive meddling I hated.

It's practically illegal to criticize a female tyrant: it's hate speech cuz all women are victims in this climate.

Separate people from the demons in em but it's still due to weakness--the strong has a hedge against em.

A female tyrant will go to war for some petty point she's making just so you'll see her as the high queen.

SWEET LITTLE LADIES UNITE!

When women are witches [not sweet little ladies] they are most vicious which they call "building bridges".

Expect empathy from a female tyrant and you'll never get it. Even a man has more feeling than those twits.

Liberal feminist: a virtue-signaler and traitor to her own race, hating her sister for having a white face.

Suddenly turning on her white sister for having privilege and giving everything to non-whites ya' see.

Women: cruelest guards in concentration camps for they are most obdurate defending wrong to the end.

The only answer is for women to become sweet little ladies again--but is this even possible friends?

WHAT CAME FIRST?

What is first--them "helping" the savage or him becoming a savage in response to the one-down system?

Suddenly turning on little brother for having male privilege then justifying girls' messes everywhere.

FALLEN CHURCHES

Wanting power but feeling powerless a feminist uses flying monkeys against you, the soon dissed.

To see their virtue-signaling is so embarrassing. Dogmatic sloganizing is the most inferior thinking.

The biggest virtue signaler was Hitler. It should be the most glaring red flag of all--please see past it sir.

Most insanity is demons from bad associations or habits. Repent and these symptoms leave: accept this.

The town slut kept saying she was a good person. She needs moral education cuz that's an oxymoron.

The stupidest thing is to let people into your house or to get into their car. Stay inaccessible, be smart.

Cuz the MINUTE you're in their car you gotta adapt to them--that's a NO NO, same with em coming in.

Superior man adapts to no one and is never imposed on. Let em in only with armed guards surroundin'

JEZEBEL MAL-ADAPTATIONS

The Jezebel begged me to get in her car and when I did [now at her mercy] she put me thru the ringer.

Once a victim of her rage I never saw her again. I could forgive her but she busted my boundaries, amen.

Get into their car or let em in your house: they start running their number on you: need guards.

The narcissist female tyrant has lots of men around her. That's part of her flying monkey superior stigma.

An artist must pay dearly for the divine gift of creative fire. The women wanted to kill me/called me a liar.

FALLEN CHURCHES

After betrayal she becomes hypervigilant and easily triggered. It's like a grenade range, for sure.

Deep inside I could hear women yelling at me. Either that or gossiping/borrowing things: I had to be free.

Imposed on and dominated by ruthless witches who don't know how to think or apply rules: snitches!

It scares me half to death to be around em. Cold, gross, mean, pompous, sensual, unempathic scum.

Only when you get boundaries do you realize you never had em before and the terrible price [war].

By denying hell and heaven the line between good and evil is gone and EVERYTHING will be allowed.

All the values in the bible will be considered DOGMAS of the corrupted church not truth from the first.

WOLVES DRESSED AS LAMBS

Like wolves dressed as lambs they will use the bible in a distorted way to keep men from God, far away.

The biblical monster Leviathan is what everyone fears: it's the STATE thru petty bureaucrats/killers.

Satan's name is Adversary--the opposite to everything God is in the struggle for the souls of men.

Belphegor is the Demon of Laziness. He seduces victims by suggesting gimmicks for getting rich.

Vanity leads to pride, arrogance and endless haughtiness. That was Lucifer so watch your self-importance.

Just as important as knowing the attributes of God is the archetypes from hell like the demons of laziness.

It's now gonna be one virus after another so it's the **END** of the social world as we know it--avoid her.

Now you can find out what I did 20 years ago about social distancing, solitude and quarantining.

They deny wrongdoing then attack you for the same--if a masochist codependent you'll accept the blame.

Jesse Lee Peterson says forgiveness releases PTSD. Guess I didn't fully forgive, I still fear those 3.

I dared to disagree with her and she had all the power. That was the beginning of the end of this girl.

PEOPLE PROBLEMS VS WORKING ON SELF

Don't bemoan the past cuz making the right choice at that time woulda been impossible--you weren't that gal.

You had no other choice since that's all you knew how to do at the time. Forget it now go on to the sublime.

The only reason you know it **NOW** is due to the bad past which pushed you to learn it--so now forget it.

You chose with what you knew then--so remorsing over it is entirely silly for it would only be that way again.

It was really beyond your control, knowing what you didn't know. Don't be paralyzed over the past/let it go.

The past: you can't change it/it couldn't have been any other way. That should relieve your guilt all day.

The more you express yourself the more conflict see, and then the more interesting your life will be.

People who don't experience conflict are those who don't express themselves. It's safe but boring/zombies.

FALLEN CHURCHES

The nail that gets hammered stands out. So by standing out through expression, expect conflict from em.

People can't label you as one thing cuz you're so multifaceted, from years overcoming conflict.

Having overcome all that you're unique and comparable to no one. Now, expressing all those sides is fun.

You become an interesting person by ALL the things that you are. It's like a recipe for a big star.

Since truth is stranger than fiction, you could never "make up" your life--a composite of multiplicity after strife.

Be ALL of those things in a unique recipe that is YOU. Remember, it's a composite and totally new.

If they can't categorize you--as an anomaly--it educates them too by opening/expanding their own view.

Being a unique composite of multifacets makes you irreplaceable so remember that when they say it.

Being your own unique composite makes it impossible for others to copy you though they may try it.

WITNESSING THE DARK SIDE

You had to go thru all of it--trudging for decades--to get to here: pure. Thesis - antithesis, then dominate.

And it was HORRIBLE seeing the other side. Yuk three times! I feel sorry for myself now, but I survived.

After coming from an orderly home it was sickening to see the effects of disorder and the kids were messers.

Due to the ACLU the thug brats rule in small towns and they know it. Don't ask me why, I can't explain it.

FALLEN CHURCHES

Grandma won't correct em since as a false Christian she forgives all things/says she didn't even see it.

You don't understand. Only the cross removes the STING of shame. That's the point, you're washed clean.

If someone complains her kids broke all of their windows, she denies all the glass on the floor.

After a period of struggle, rebirth.

One of the greatest delusions of salvation is a fixation on religious activity or "feeling spiritual"--it lulls.

Looking back at all the obstacles shows great danger but God took ya thru them all without realizing it sir.

If people are willing to turn on their neighbors and shoot em in a ditch they can certainly backstab/switch.

Cuz I didn't want to hangout they wanted to kill me. That's a social generation, taking it as an insult/blasphemy.

Fast for five days. Join the elite by not-doing. It's easy and quite a relief and deep rest from everyday living.

IT WAS HORRIBLE LIVING WITH LIBERALS

It was horrible living with a buncha liberals cuza their dirty minds. If you love dogs they'll say it's bestiality.

They have dirty minds and accuse others of what they are doing. It's always that way and it's been frustrating.

We the decent have been attacked from all sides. And it's been decades and continuing now as it increases.

They'll immediately call you friend and that brings obligations--miss em and they'll crack down.

You're not their friend/you're their slave.

FALLEN CHURCHES

A Dionysian generation is social also. The self-disciplined man is a loner and persecuted by the low.

I was shocked in kindergarten and more shocked thru all the grades and even college, esp. graduate school.

They were sickening and terrifying and I didn't want to go to school. Later on to adapt I just used alcohol.

Excuse me, you remind me of someone I used to know. Arrogant, a plagiarist and a dam fool know it all.

What gives you the right to decide the subtlety of MY work? What makes you so superior, ask that first.

I call it SUBTLE cuz it's a STYLE I've been GIVEN and only I can describe it, like Johannesse Verse twit.

Build it, they will come. God will draw em to it and it'll be massive/a large sum.

Just cuz I forgave you'all doesn't mean I won't write about you or use you as an example of raging wolves.

What is a real man? He pays the bills and protects me/our home and that's the bottom line for millennium.

A home is not just walls but an amalgamation of personalities, their DNA, it is everything to me.

STOP WASTING TIME

If they're not helping you to ultimate goals forget em. Time is the essence-- don't bounce around in reaction.

People just wanna hang out or use you as a pit stop. If you wanna create empire you can't have this: NOT.

Before I stopped the reactive life--living from interruption to interruption--they were coming day and night.

FALLEN CHURCHES

I'm never bored/lonely and work all the time. They're bored and lonely so seek me as their supply, prime.

By becoming an interesting person with multifacets you're gonna have to draw boundaries or lose all that.

A Dionysian generation is social also. The self-disciplined man is a loner and persecuted by the low.

I'm never bored/lonely and work all the time. They're bored and lonely so seek me as their supply, prime.

Working on yourself always works. You attract better partners and resist enmeshment with jerks.

Part of the reason we get stuck in cycles is we don't value time enough. I won't allow it for a minute, I'm off.

You get stuck with people who really don't care about you. A total waste of time, losers in the darkness, pooh.

Jerks who play games, disappear to keep you on your toes or ghost you, having learned that works ya' know.

"Keep em on their toes by keeping em confused" is the game and it's a waste of time for the muse.

You are FREE in Christ to have a beautiful productive creative life, yet you need him/her--more strife?

He/she makes you feel BAD. This is not of God it's of the world and reflective of a part of you that's flawed.

DON'T GO TO THEIR PAGES!

Go to his page/channel you'll hear a shit-shot to keep you in line or make you feel vulnerable--AGAIN.

You don't need this. Stay in the circumstances God has given you, do your work, pull in, pet your kittens.

FALLEN CHURCHES

Pull into YOUR situation--in "SITU"--for happiness. The internet has distorted our reality and I regressed.

As we get older, time is far more important. Avoid the social time wasters, they are everywhere.

The minute you're embroiled in drama with some fella, pull back into your own SITU, you've got work to do.

If you valued time more you would not WASTE it on things and people that don't serve you. Be gone, whew!

Why waste time with people who are happy to waste your time? When on the phone, they go on and on...

Why waste time with people who don't care anything about you? Have aristocratic reserve, to you be true.

Do these people care about you? NO? Why waste your time with them then? Masochists are blue.

When you're with em they say something that sticks in your craw. You chew it for days: be gone.

A deep empath can't afford to be involved with this crap. Be done with it, make your TIME your map.

This social hypnotic madness of not letting anyone work in solitude has permeated the churches and it's rude.

INDEPENDENCE IS ANATHAMA

If you don't go to their boring pot lucks they take it upon themselves to come to your door and confront.

If you don't go to their boring socials it means you hate God himself--that's the modern church ya' know.

They don't admire someone with a life project working all the time in private-- he doesn't have a right to exist!

FALLEN CHURCHES

They don't admire independence and commitment to higher goals but only social conformity with foes.

Fortunately I transcended the problem and figured it out--God loved me even if I was an anti-social gal.

I had to fight liberalism in the churches--like the "all is one" heresy--and in all cases they were worldly.

The Americana values are independence and autonomy--not loyalty to the group, the only value conformity.

Others without my background can't see the problem and just sink in their swill, thinking God abandoned em.

The Latter Days is the era of the false church and preachers from hell and the churches are SOCIAL.

So both the secular and the church is a waste of time. You have God's work to do and it's creatively sublime.

There is so LITTLE time if you have big dreams. You must spend all your energy on them every minute it seems.

Earlier I trusted people and lost my independence, being at their mercy. This taught me EVERYTHING, see?

DON'T EVER GO WITH EM

I won't go anywhere with em in a car cuz then I'm at their mercy. When in power they may get weird, see?

You're not gonna screw with my head anymore! I'm not gonna be at your mercy, man--it's a bore.

I've got better things to do, man--like a Creative Act by God, an actual structure in nature I've developed.

So I'm gonna let you sink in your noncreative swill while I pull back into what I know, my HOME [my pill].

FALLEN CHURCHES

No I'm not going anywhere with you. I have a driver. No I'm not going to stay with you. I'll get a hotel.

You gotta cut people outa your life. You need to spend every minute working to your goals, so high.

If they don't care anything about you nor bring any value to your life, CUT THEM OUT--do it now.

I wasted much of my early life being nice when users came to the door. If you're not assertive, you're a LOSER.

The reason you're having people problems is you don't value time enough. You let em in the house?

They make you their bitch by beginning with threats [you don't treat me good enough] then you submit.

They make you their bitch by calling you their friend and then demanding you act in ways that suit them.

This is the fallen church and society. When independence and autonomy reigned you didn't have this, see?

Whether liberal thugs or church fuzz people act like they own you and RESENT--big time--your independence.

Their resentment at my independence drove me into solitude years back and I've decided it's the gist.

BE NICE IS CULTURAL DECLINE

The whole "be nice" or "it's all good" thing shows an evil person adapting to the current cultural decline.

He can't form a line, he can't divide from them. He swam in muddy waters and still has mud on him.

He wants to have a foot in both camps, still maintaining a hold but since this can't be done, he fades.

FALLEN CHURCHES

You don't support me enough, you don't do this or that enough--omg! Here it comes, manipulation.

It's always one thing: You're not doing enough. It's always on you--never on them cuz you're happy alone.

People make big trouble. Don't let em come around anymore--you're outa grace with the Lord.

They let your dog outa the gate and said they didn't know. Stupid stuff--there's always something: let em GO!

It's YOU--YOU, YOU, YOU: YOU are not doing enough. When it gets like this, be done/be off.

Then it happens again, for a different reason. Then it happens again, for a different reason: this is human.

When Susan came around it was one mishap after another. Such a waste of time--let em in, you will blunder.

When Shane came around it was one favor after another. He'd charm his way in then ask for whatever.

I wasted so much time with people who cared nothing or didn't know of my work/destiny. No more frenemies.

People hold you back/rarely help you up. Social addiction is needing em more while enjoying em less: yuk!

BY GETTING ENTANGLED

By getting entangled with em they distort your thinking cuz your emotions are involved--don't go there, seclude.

If you're depressed, drill down: WHO were you around? Ignore appearances, there are wolves in town.

We're not built for guilt but people wanna lay it on you and that's when you draw your boundaries: be gone.

FALLEN CHURCHES

Women are the worst as they relapse into virtue signaling about everything, making you look bad and ugly.

It's best to break it off with someone like that. Let em find some other supply who just likes to hangout.

Michelle was a total user. Women can be terrible imposers especially if narcissists. Draw lines, resist, insist.

The narcissist needs constant stimulation and gets bored easily. Perhaps that's why you feel replaced, silly.

The narc can't feel stimulated by normal things that keep others content. They're constantly searchin'.

The narcissist moves on/replaces you quickly because he always has backup supplies.

If he's a narcissist, you were one of many--so when the discard occurs he's already with somebody.

HANDLING DISRESPECT

You have a stronger identity after walking away from disrespect and it takes skill to learn it quick.

It's damaging to your soul to be disrespected. You must immediately do something once you notice it.

Being disrespected can cause depression and physical ailments. Do yourself a huge favor and get this.

Disrespect: If you're not noticing it or not fighting against it, forget it--your life takes a downturn to the pits.

Our psyches are not created to be disrespected and we're not built for guilt. These are maladies to quit.

We're created to have dignity and to love our true self and that means PROTECTING ourselves.

FALLEN CHURCHES

This healthy self-protection means keeping yourself free of toxic situations and people: darkness/evil.

Whenever you protect yourself from disrespect it gives you self-respect but if you don't you end in a ditch.

No matter who it is, you must now get a backbone. They're disgusted and your weakness is showin'.

They disrespected me by their very presence. The way they walked right in, the arrogance, the invasiveness.

She disrespected me by her very presence--of wanting everything I have and am, running Jezebel scams.

Wanting a piece of me--that's what it feels like. The public school's communist "sharing" spirit: yikes!

They want everything I have/I don't have a right to it. It's "not fair"--from Americana we've fallen so far.

They're so grabby and mean--the sucking spirit taking everything not nailed down--I never wanna see em.

The way they target what they want is so objectifying you feel like a grunt and end up saying "where is love?"

My invaders were high school class of '85--horrible, evil, violent--so what are they like now? Hate to think.

Of course that was California, an evil liberal communist state. In middle America they're more decent.

WHAT THEY PUT ME THROUGH

What they put me through, having no limits. I had so much to learn and I had to learn it fast, or death.

Next was the Harry Potter generation, even worse. These are the pagan females destroying the church.

FALLEN CHURCHES

It's the sucking spirit saying what's yours is mine or you're a hateful person refusing to share: "it's not fair".

Now it's gangster culture and anything goes no matter how low--your best friend will decapitate you now.

You don't have to be rude about it, just calmly say "that behavior is not ok with me, it's disrespectful, ok?"

I love vocabulary words, I love expressing myself in terse verse, I love doing God's work: that comes first. END END

It hurts so much deep in my soul to be disrespected. Believe me, it's a mighty important subject.

Unwarranted disrespect can lead to decades long addictions, all based on something confusin'

When you sense it--something else you gotta learn or retrieve it--you must confront it or regret it.

PH.D. IN THE STREETS

Besides formal education I got a "Ph.D. in the Streets": learning how people gang up/how they cheat.

I was their victim in liberal California where young thugs take over small towns and get away with it all.

If they disrespect your privacy that's a travesty but few demand it since the social is superior you see.

Only the rich know they have a right to privacy, few demand it fearing neediness in an emergency.

They made me feel I didn't have a right to pick my own friends. It was imposed on me, that's the trend.

WHY they're disrespectful is not your problem. They could be a narcissist, jealous, distracted--so what?

FALLEN CHURCHES

The only thing you can control is the boundaries you set--who you let in. You MUST do this, and be firm.

You can control the distance you put between you and another person--and know cuza that it's over.

It takes skill and knowledge to recognize the signs of disrespect and as time goes on they're more minute.

It takes skill to know enough to walk away from it, for they're people we care about, but there's loss.

Don't blame yourself for your brash reactions to disrespect or that's another hook into the culprits.

What we need is NURTURING and that's not possible when being disrespected. See these as opposites.

You can have a disrespecter as an acquaintance but they can't get close anymore--it's self-abandonment.

When it comes to family dinners at holidays in situations when they disrespected you, it's a NO-GO.

When my heart yells "NO" I respect my intuition and truth and move back away from potential blues.

FRIENDLESS CAN BE BLISS

As scary as it is to be friendless in the interim, nothing feels as good as self-respect, no kiddin' hon'.

You're tired of being disrespected by someone constantly crossing your boundaries after you said it.

I didn't know this, I had to learn it the hard way. I never knew I should demand respect or walk away.

Shame is an important topic when considering narcissistic abuse. It erodes self-esteem/blocks good sense.

FALLEN CHURCHES

Stop over-analyzing something so simple to understand. You're there for them, they're not for you, done.

When people care about you they'll go out of their way, oh yah! But these people won't lift a finger at all.

Instead of convoluting your thoughts, simplify things by knowing: they don't care about you, so let go.

Most of the narcissist's actions are emotional, not logical. When you're a fresh supply, they idolize you gal.

They'll use many reasons to discard you but the real reason is: their emotions changed/now they dis.

They felt "injured" cuz you lessened their supply or weren't there in a minute. So they discard, deal with it.

As he runs low on supplies the narc will re-idealize you. He misses your special brand or something new.

They use excuses to justify their erratically changing emotions based on full vs. dwindling supply.

When they find someone new to replace you they'll have reasons for the switch but all irrelevant too.

Learn the art of being alone to become a stronger and more powerful person. Learn that then attract em.

APPROVAL-GETTING

Approval getting: Not "what can I do to make him like me" but "what can he do to make me like him": new setting.

Stop seeking the approval of others. They should be proving to YOU they're worth it or whatever.

Stop doing things for them to gain people's approval. They should be getting YOURS--remember that now.

Make that self-loving switch in your mind and you'll be amazed at your past stupidity being "kind".

How much better life is when you see people caring about you and seeking YOUR approval: GET THIS.

It's a totally different mindset and so relieving. Now you're on your way to a successful life producing.

It's better to go home and watch your favorite shows than to go so low as to seek approval from those.

Make this switch and life will be INFINITELY better--you'll see a radically different image in the mirror.

It made me sick seeing you wanting his approval. What a waste of time and self-esteem for you, a jewel.

Always come from a position of strength/power--meaning you can walk away anytime, a real mover.

HE'S NOT THAT INTO YOU

It's so much easier to say he has a narcissistic disorder than to admit he just found someone better.

He's not that into you. He comes around when he's bored but then goes away again: wakeup or stay blue.

Push, pull: come-here-go-away behavior may not be a disorder but just one thing: he doesn't care.

It's much easier on the ego to call him a narcissist gamer than to say "he just doesn't care".

It's about INTEREST every time. Make yourself interesting and stop making excuses analyzing the guy.

When discarded it's easy to call him a narcissist--when what happened was he just found someone else.

FALLEN CHURCHES

Just because they found someone they like more than you doesn't make em a narcissistic maniac: let em go.

Being discarded isn't always narcissistic behavior. It happens all the time with favor and desire.

Push and pull means low interest, discard means found someone better, comes back: lonely or whatever.

It's confusing when words say one thing but behavior something else. Actions have meaning, words don't.

The fool takes words at face value but the wise girl knows: words don't mean a thing until they show it.

See the absurdity: You miss me so much but I never see you. Put their words with actions to be happy.

SEE how much their words don't mean anything. They are empty, disproven by behavior you're scrutinizing.

It's very simple: If you love someone you're there for them, do things for them--not just throw em crumbs.

He says "I love you" to feel good about himself but then it all disperses as he puts you back on the shelf.

WORDS OR ACTIONS

The way they treat you totally determines whether their words mean anything. Stop hearing/start looking.

They tell you things to get your attention and to make sure their supplies are there whenever they need em.

Stop saying what he said--his actions are what are true. Words are cheap so start being a relationship sleuth.

Look at what they DO and then determine if they care about you--and then it's so bloody obvious too.

They can't hide it for long. They can B.S. with words but not with actions and you'll wake up to a new song.

LOVEBOMBING AND FUTURE-FAKING

The narcissist wants to plant the idea they're in for the long haul. During lovebombing it's "future faking".

He's lovebombing and wants to take you on a fabulous trip--don't do it or be at anyone's mercy chick.

A narcissist calls you his "soul mate" right before devaluing. Get used to flip-flops with him.

When he needs supply it's "you're the one for me"--it's hard to hear that and walk away, but do it sweetie.

Don't make the extremely dangerous choice to hang on--to stay one more day, a little bit longer to ice.

For when he discards, life is mentally and emotionally hard and it takes time. Don't let this happen!

A narcissist isn't looking for "the one" but the one who satisfies them in the moment--RUN!

MOM GOT MAD

Mom got mad at me for liking dad again. It's the mind-rape we're discussing: heart pain, division, manipulation.

Shared custody with narcs makes life miserable. The kids copy him or become empathetic doormats, ya know?

There's only two results: become like the narc parent or refuse to be that way and become the opposite.

Why is it so hard to forgive the mother? Cuz the victims went into denial long ago, it must be uncovered.

FALLEN CHURCHES

She seems so victimized by the whole thing but as a liberal feminist it's pure lies and dogma she's instilling.

Hypnotized by a feminist there's future therapy they're gonna need for years even decades, I know it.

She makes you hate men and the boy becomes beta in fear of showing any characteristics of the masculine.

I see skinny beta men everywhere and you can bet they were raised by a feminist, without a prayer.

The feminist narrative is mother-raised beta males are nicer to women: no, they're just scared of em.

They put the girls FIRST to put the little boys in their place. They even do it to male dogs--what a disgrace!

Do a search on how narcissists treat their children. You'll see the system and the disaster of being fallen.

You KNOW it doesn't feel right when he says it day and night. It helps to know it's basic to this blight.

Forgive em but don't be their victim. Don't hang in to help them, forgetting you always get the short end.

SUCCESS

The only reason for failure is excuses, for it doesn't matter how old you are, how rich/poor or feeling helpless.

The only way you can do what you're supposed to do is be yourself--not from copying others which is hell.

Your job is to be YOU--the best you can be--and that will be your greatest success but it takes courage.

Being YOU is NEW: something that has never been done before. It's a discovery of the ages, brand new.

FALLEN CHURCHES

It has nothing to do with age/money but just one thing: the **COURAGE** to be yourself, utterly ravishing.

Being **YOU** is **NEW**: something that has never been done before--a discovery of the ages and so cute.

There are good people but they don't call themselves "good"--they just live well/act as they should.

Narc says "I love you" a million times while you're love bombed and beyond: it kicks his game into motion.

I'm happy that no matter how immature, sinful, crazy--you're eternally grateful for the truth I gave thee.

I'm a poli-psych poet. It's political as psychology extends into the public domain and it surely shows it.

They're killing pets in China. Stupid heathen--you don't have to kill dogs and cats, just don't **EAT** them!

The feminist narrative is: mother-raised beta males are nicer to women--no, they're just scared of em.

It's the 112th book and I feel good about the form it took, starting with fallen churches, ending with crooks.

It helps to know past actors you hanker over were archetypes: easily replaced/no more that way.

DEPLATIONS AND HUMILATIONS

He deflated, losing all self confidence suddenly. Though it hurts, recall that triumph follows humiliation.

For His spirit to come thru God's gotta keep you humble. He'll put a thorn in your side, just to keep you small.

Sometimes you gotta friggin' eat crow. I know how it hurts, a lifetime thinking something which is false.

FALLEN CHURCHES

It's incredibly beneficial to go thru this. The humiliation, public or otherwise, is a necessary phase.

For your creativity to be SO BIG He's gotta keep you small cuz that 'ol ego will end it ALL.

Let em flatter/complement you, don't you let it go to your head! Cuz that ends all potential, be a vessel instead.

Fix your life now, ask for God's help. He can realign it in a minute and take you out of hell.

I lost my grant with the medical school when I said I was a vessel. Experienced too not just fluff and folderol.

The fact I experienced all this crap doesn't mean I didn't book learn it too but that's the science view.

I didn't agree with their "scientific" views like vivisection is ok, or alcoholics can learn to drink again [then die].

Then I met and dated a male psychologist who totally screwed my head up, requiring therapy.

This man was actually the chief of staff and a total sadist. All I can say is: don't mess with people's minds.

No I have no faith in the psych profession or academia. The stories I could tell would surely shame ya.

They use their high positions to seduce young women and their behavior is shameless in that status.

SMART WOMEN ARE TARGETED

A smart woman is likely to stand out intellectually and that's enough to make her targeted daily.

There's no way I could keep up the shine or the stoke going, they brought me down—paper airplanes flown.

FALLEN CHURCHES

All over pronouns--I couldn't handle the audience. The pronoun thing were speedbumps, I was highest.

When I said "mankind" or "he" as a nonpersonal pronoun referring to all humans, they'd yell "he and she".

It's this kinda obstruction that screwed my mind up. I couldn't handle the audience, I had to build up.

Look at the flack Jordan Peterson takes, refusing to succumb to their stupid pronoun demands.

Who needs a public presence in this era? Just create your content and retire/find some way to be separate.

Things are gonna heat up like you can't believe. Can't hold back a tidal wave, I'd just be planning to leave.

And that's what you're sensing: the humiliation is actually the OVERWHELMING feeling of what we face.

Without the sound you can appreciate the fine artistry of EVERY SCENE--they are delicately brilliant.

Awareness is like cracking an egg and it can physically hurt but then after DEBUNK it's RECONSTRUCT.

NARCISSISTIC PROJECTIONS IN FAMILY SYSTEMS

Narcissists can't deal with negative emotions so those closest soak em up like a sponge.

Once a negative emotion sponge you take projections personally and if no boundaries = tragedy.

If you were early taught to receive these negative emotions then you will do this as an adult = become a nut.

Narcs love to pull people in their midst who are WILLING to take responsibility for these--and be pissed.

FALLEN CHURCHES

Narcs can't own these emotions themselves--they MUST find surrogates to push em all out.

They must find sponges to ACT OUT emotions--they lash out or attack until they do, daughters or sons.

Mom gets drunk and up comes all this alien crap she can't handle so she projects it onto you to deal with.

She'd bang on dad's bedroom door all afternoon--he'd be locked in--then make sure I hated him too.

Biggest effects of boundaryless members is introjection and projection: one big mass of haters.

One can't walk into this maelstrom and straighten it all out--the answer is individuation/working on themselves.

Very good you can see this. You're smart, a lucky one. Most grow up passive-aggressive tornados ready to burst out.

Mom gets relief by you acting out HER fears. You're merged together--that explains your insanity dear.

Why were you crazy in your twenties? It wasn't you--it was pure introjection before you separated from insanity.

When you SEPARATE [individuate] that's when the real reverberations occur, but continue getting clear.

With separation from the mass system it can be terrifying. You don't have them or yourself yet, but persevere.

INDIVIDUATION PANIC/SEPARATION ANXIETY

Suddenly you don't know your own family and you're an alien to THEM. I pity you if you can't get out then.

I thought I knew them but I DIDN'T. They seemed to hate me suddenly like I was a stranger, an alien.

FALLEN CHURCHES

The worst thing possible is to get drunk or do drugs at this point. Know what is happening: God will anoint.

When part of the mass, things went on smoothly and I never questioned it. Now, it was WAR and I knew it.

Being part of the mass family system--undifferentiated--is the basis of schizophrenia, compulsions, addictions.

But without family support--and not yet strong going solo--can tear you apart. Seek therapy ol' sport.

As an adult without a STRONG sense of self, you're prone to soak up negative emotions and continue hell.

As an adult you'll WANT to soak it up since that's your identity all along and it distracts--feels good.

Getting bored: When things are going smoothly she isn't happy and has to start a WAR out of nowhere.

Her recurrent alcohol binges brought relief--here we go again, a distraction from our family disease.

Parents may be a Gruesome Twosome, welded together forever with their fights the glue or whatever.

Was on SRIs for two weeks and was affected for decades after. The problem is the family not you lover.

REFUSE TO RECEIVE: THE WAY OUT

The way out is to refuse to receive these emotions. You being affected by devaluation proves you are man.

They gotta devalue you so you'll play out emotions they can't handle: making you angry, creating scandal.

So-and-so told me this about you, people are asking me why I even like you, la de da: make you BLUE.

FALLEN CHURCHES

She knows exactly what buttons to push, it's part of the system game that maintains itself: the status quo.

Narcissist moms can't tolerate seeing themselves in a negative light. They gotta project to feel right.

Narcs are perfectionists–they can't tolerate seeing themselves that way. If you play bad, hurray.

Mom was a perfectionist who felt under-appreciated. Never mind twice a week she was a raving lunatic.

When healthy [separate] you'll say: "Ok, throw your fit, I'm not gonna pay any attention to it. I'm whole, legit."

It's the whole key: you don't wanna RECEIVE. It starts with awareness and creating a bubble of separateness.

You have to be AWARE people do this and it's actually happening. It affects neurons, inner mappings.

I got emails trying to push my buttons and trigger me for years but geographic relocation saved the seer.

"WE don't believe you wrote a book" and when I wrote 110 I never heard from them again, but not forsook.

It's always "WE" like they're a happy system and you're the alien. "We" was a trigger but now I love being alone.

I'VE GRADUATED

I've graduated: I don't have to care if someone else is mad, it has nothing to do with me and I can even be glad.

Once you know who you are and become aware, it doesn't affect you now. You don't go near, you just know.

Now this will occur in social environments, unless you're a hermit like me. A social isolate: that's the epitome.

FALLEN CHURCHES

After disentangling from the sick system mass attractions were immediate but I'm still an isolate.

As an adult, look out for negative emotions being projected onto you or you'll feel like crap with a loony map.

Scientists are told: don't you dare talk about the virus or biosludge, you'll lose your job or be smudged.

If the virus breaks out in Mexico you'll have a flood into the US and they'll go to sanctuary cities = epic tragedy.

If Mexico can't control drug cartels how will they control the pandemic? Not likely--they'll flood our cities.

We just found the virus is in human feces. When they go to Frisco it'll spread like wildfire: epic pandemic.

A nation not controlling borders can't control a pandemic. Open borders ensures it: sanctuary cities most hit.

Survivors of coronavirus will be scarred for life: massive heart/lung problems and secondary infections.

GOODBYE SANCTUARY CITIES

They discovered the caronavirus is present in human feces--goodbye sanctuary cities.

HIV included in virus delivery system? Why is big tech suppressing this news of biblical proportions?

No I can NOT make commitments since I never know when the line will come THRU me, I'm always busy.

No, I don't wanna talk on the phone. There's too much interruption, talking over, waiting. Email please.

When we talk on the phone, I'm your slave--having to adapt to you, your dullness, the emptiness.

FALLEN CHURCHES

Thank you Shane, Chris, Larry, Michelle, Susan and Cindy--you were my Ph.D. in the Streets and 110 books.

I cried me a bucket cuz I got involved with you nuts and went down a rabbit hole of evil and empty ruts.

You imposed on me so much tho' I see now it was your emptiness and seeking solutions, but tough.

All I can say is the devil made me do it--my whole life, due to weakness. But now I'm strong and he's out of it.

The system explains why I went crazy, there was no other explanation. Then add SRIs = demons.

I feel I'm being carried in a stream, in spite of myself. It's a higher thing now, outa me and my measly help.

Many more helpers are involved now: virtual assistants, promoters, aestheticians and even plastic surgeons.

I couldn't mess it up if I tried. I'd be letting down so many people on the outside attracted into mine.

I've noticed if I have music on the dogs don't demand to go out and play ball so much, just at lunch.

It's all about why we can't leave our house but meanwhile the borders are wide open North and South.

THE GIST OF THE THEORY

Sick society is a turkey shoot. The harvest is ripe for a moral revolution or evangelism: it's a cakewalk.

The gist: people are like crabs in a bucket keeping each other down. I'm impressed with very few of em.

He thinks he's so great it's embarrassing. In truth he has little to say or makes a big deal outa nothing.

FALLEN CHURCHES

If you feel bad after going to his page/show its cuz it's not **TRUTH** tho' he says it is, or it's beside the point.

The smartest thing my mentor ever said was "don't go to their pages". There's a problem so avoid it.

Van Gogh and Gauguin argued constantly about painting. I don't like community, I'd rather be solo writing.

I prayed God would give me something to do so He put a Creative Act inside me and it took decades too.

He's popular in his dumbed down position--good for him--but I prefer profundity not the peanut gallery.

As people get older some get nicer, some get meaner, some return to who they were before being a faker.

HE'S NOT YOUR FRIEND!

First, see he's not your friend. That's a giant one, it'll get you far--so loving thoughts can't intrude again.

The chances are extremely high that if you can't **LET GO** then he's a narcissist/you're a codependent.

Stop projecting onto people that they care about you. **YOU** care but they're walking out the door.

The grief you feel with mistreatment is what you needed to feel at early trauma but can cry out now.

A schema is what we believe about ourselves. Self-hate finds enemies who prove we're bad/it's hell.

These core mal-adaptive schemas are the **BLUEPRINTS** of our life-view and determine who we attract too.

Social isolation and alienation is the schema feeling you don't belong. It's not you just the early song.

FALLEN CHURCHES

Taught they were incompetent, another maladaptive schema is needing help when it's not needed.

If someone makes you miserable feeling bad about yourself he's not right for you/you'll be blue.

Obvious truth making one blue: If someone makes you feel like crap he's not right for you.

It's not so much about him but the stability and lifestyle he enables for us. Stable homelife = happiness.

If only women could see this. They're being protected and supported yet still complaining--feminists.

She says husband isn't exciting--yet he's enabling a life where she can create her own excitement.

SECURITY RELEASES CREATIVITY

Protection and security releases creativity in a woman. She should be grateful for that not complainin.

When I think of how I was constantly bothered by people --like I had a bulls eye on me--I'd hate to be single.

They would NOT leave me alone. It was like they were jealous of my solitude, the basis of my throne.

It makes em angry if they can't control you. Living in a cabin/ghost town compelled them to intrude.

It felt like the whole universe wanted to control me. I only wanted to escape the undertow and be free.

I knew they didn't understand me. What would these losers understand about the ivory tower?

I married 13 years ago and all intrusions stopped. No one ever bothered me again, I was free, AMEN!

FALLEN CHURCHES

I was finally free of losers like you, narcissists who play to the peanut gallery, wanting attention: go away.

God said: Keep writing. Someone will read it after your death. It's about the copy not what others saith.

My mind can't tolerate contradictions. Before writing it out [in brutal reversals] I was just an angry nut.

Stop being so forgiving/letting it slide every time. People know exactly what they're doing. Tom Hardy

God said: I know what you've been thru--I was there too--but it was necessary while on the potter's wheel.

FALLEN CHURCHES LOVE LOSERS

FALLEN CHURCHES is why we hang on to losers: never told right from wrong, friends from lechers

High and mighty one minute and mowed down like grass the next. No one gets out alive that's the gist.

Addiction Hex: It was an attachment trauma, a broken bond that leaked into the biological--food/sex.

Depending on the level of energy at birth, the mal-adaptation is magnified into an extreme curse.

The extremity of his perverse addiction reflects the level of **TRAUMA** with the broken bond connection.

His pure sadism reflects the sadism of his rejector since everything noxious gets repeated on another.

The only way to stop repetition compulsion is to drill down and go back, giving yourself the love you lacked.

Without a strong sense of God/the true church we fall back into mal-adaptive schemas which screw us.

FALLEN CHURCHES

They had no idea how to act since their parents were clueless hippies too: emulate docs of WWII.

How could they have moral guidelines when their parents were always talking about sex with NO lines?

They accepted dirty jokes in the home. This set the stage for lawless sexuality seen before the fall of Rome.

If they'd had moral guidelines in a true church they'd see their sinful parents and transcend the curse.

EFFECTS OF THE FALLEN CHURCH

What is the true church? The body of believers not a building/local body--you must TEST the spirits.

I'll never forget when Pastor got restraining orders from liberal imposers--substituting for father/mother.

Pastor substituted for father by blocking Shane, Susan, Cindy, Michelle and Craig: the walking dead.

When wicked man said "I love sex" Christian lady felt offense, saying "that's none of my business".

When a wicked man says that to a woman it's a shit-shot testing response and must be punished.

That's the kind of thing you tell pastor--so he can visit that wicked man and banish the lecher.

It helps to recognize the magnitude of the problem of broken bonds/attachment trauma: it's common.

We're all screwed up with emotional illness from maternal feminists but most solve it thru social-ness.

Well I couldn't be social as my cure, I had to go into solitude with just dogs and cats to feel secure.

FALLEN CHURCHES

Being so screwed up by mom I suppose it's easy to slide into a social illness of chit-chat and laziness.

But I admire drive, tenacity, discipline, early nights and getting up before dawn to start all over again.

I can't wait to hit the computer and see what's happening. I've had it with petty dramas/schemas around me.

FEMINIST MOMS

Feminist moms are liberal by default. They call It "loving" but it's opposite, that's what divorce is all about.

To feminist moms it's a self-evident truth that you're crazy and they're not: there's no arguing with these nuts.

Ok, I'm staying out of moral duty. But that makes me right with God and that's a WIN-WIN in the end buddy.

To the wicked man who said "I love sex": Pastor told me to tell you that's NONE OF MY BUSINESS.

Child/pet neglecters can't see the beauty of God's creation which unfolds when you love them.

No Christian shall be condemned. Why not just wait for that miracle and forget what happened?

SEASON OF TREASON

In my season of treason God lowered the hedge and evil flowed in, cuz w/out God it's the default setting.

To rid past resentments see your life longitudinally in phases: You were down now you're a success.

See your life longitudinally/phasically: You were in a bootcamp with an A-hole D.I., now you're high.

FALLEN CHURCHES

The drill instructor was public opinion when you were fallen and sister gossips before you stood up.

Why is everyone told to smile? It's silly and fake. No other generation acted like this: "cheesecake".

People who went thru WWII and the depression got their priorities right. This generation is a blight.

To get to here you had to go through a bootcamp. It was hell growing up but necessary, now forget it.

It was just a shit-shot to test response and needs to be punished. Walk away gently and banish at once.

A bad memory ruins the moment but if we see it as just an early phase we see it in context: bootcamp.

Globalism is being dominated by some bureaucrat. He lays down the silly rules and you can't say squat.

The more local the politics the more it's just you. We don't want globalism where we can't say pooh.

The narc will feel you're a stage 5 "clinger" in a couple days not months like most--he's a changer.

EARLY TRAUMAS BECOME BLUEPRINTS

Due to early trauma we fear being abandoned, see people as unreliable and choose the same "thrill".

With any maladaptive schema [roadmap] we'll pick bad people: repetition compulsion to fail.

If we BELIEVE something about ourselves [schema] we must PROOVE it on a daily basis tho' it kills ya.

The horrible thing about schema-blueprints is you'll pull those towards you who will cheat/lie in a minute.

FALLEN CHURCHES

If you always expect to get the short end of the stick it's a result of early trauma of extreme negligence.

They're always in victim mode, in positions of being used all because they expect nothing BUT abuse.

It's amazing to heal from these maladaptive schemas. They rule our life and it's hell, I attest to this.

You assume things will go wrong cuz they always have. But that was your preparation stage/bootcamp.

Liberalism has messed up our psychologies since the sixties. We lost our moral compass to be trendy.

We walk into a church and are not on equal ground with the others who end up demolishing us.

MALADAPTIVE SCHEMAS

One maladaptive schema comes from emotional deprivation--never expecting it from anyone.

This is a life showing absence of attention, warmth, companionship, empathy, understanding.

With one caught in this schema there is no mutual sharing with others. Like the old west, picture it.

There is an absence of strength, counsel or guidance from others. Now how does this happen--mothers?

The formation of an identity embroiled with emotional deprivation or expectation? Unmet needs at one.

Unmet needs as a child creates the emotionally deprived maladaptive schema of the neurotic adult.

Defective [SHAME] schema: the feeling one is inferior, bad or insignificant to others.

One result is hypersensitivity to criticism/blame or social awkwardness--from others I must hide my mess.

This child was never made to feel competent, capable or having efficacy. That's now his roadmap, see?

He wasn't appreciated for just being alive, a unique spirit. And without this imputed self-worth, forget it.

Feeling emotionally deprived, starting to build identity, getting needs met = finally satisfied/satiated.

With intensity of the early trauma, rejection brings an explosion. Drill back down, be the loved one.

Insecurity/unwanted way back then becomes: If anyone got to know me they'd see how defective I am.

INTENSITY OF EARLY TRAUMA

If unwanted as a child the schema will be SKEWED and maladaptive-- interaction with the world is bad.

Feelings of the unwanted: isolated from the rest of the world, different from others, not part of a group.

Unwanted situation: a person who's walking around with a gaping wound in complete social isolation.

This type of alienation is a horribly painful way to live. I can attest to this until reclusion was appreciated.

I saw my differences, how I just wanted solitude and how they were socially adapted and rather crude.

There is healing for this! You understand who you are and that you are love, that you didn't deserve the dis.

Schema: Incompetence. The belief one can't handle everyday responsibilities, feeling like a dunce.

FALLEN CHURCHES

Even when I was doing fine, in fact splendidly, I felt helpless requiring the assistance of others.

One must grieve the loss of not being properly instructed and built then love your self cuz no one else will.

Schema: vulnerability to harm/illness. An exaggerated fear disaster will strike any time/the future's hellish.

Catastrophe fears: mental, going crazy. physical: die of cancer. Outer: collapsing elevator/damned future.

PAINFUL SCHEMAS CAN BE HEALED

This constant fear of imminent disaster leads to suicide after a life of continuous dread and terror.

It leads to self-harm, drinking, promiscuity, horrible things. Imagine it: a life like horror movies.

Living through maladaptive schemas is painful but it can be **HEALED**. Just these words alone can reveal.

Thinking that you're going to be hurt is a painful way to live. I used to feel that way every minute.

Schema: **ENMESHMENT** with a sick system at the expense of individuation or normal socialization.

The one enmeshed shows emptiness, floundering, having no direction or questions his existence.

AWARENESS IS THE SOLUTION

AWARENESS is so big here. If you see you have one of these maladaptive schemas you're almost there.

"That's why my abusive relationships, feeling unworthy of love, why I can't keep a job and sabotage myself."

The feeling that one is a failure, incompetent, stupid, less successful than others, insignificant: how awful!

Entitlement/grandiosity is the mal-adaptive schema of the narcissist and that's been explained in these books.

Schema: Lack of self-control/self-discipline. Overeating, addiction, bottomless pit syndrome, grasping.

Inability to restrain impulses or emotional self-expressions necessary for success: they have none of this.

Schema: Exaggerated emphasis on avoiding any discomfort, pain, exertion, responsibility, conflict.

Schemas: subjugation, approval/recognition-seeking, self-sacrifice, pessimism, perfectionism.

Drill down, go back to your child, love yourself cuz no one else did, build back up, find true love and success.

Once thinking you married the wrong person/met the right one the idea of divorce takes root: bliss is gone.

Sometimes I'd feel like he was taking me over--not subjugated, except insofar as I was baited.

The interchangeability with narcissists is cuz people are seen only in terms of UTILITY, not "you" sweetie.

Because the narcissist knows nothing about himself he must invent false identities just to feel he exists.

CHRONIC EMPTINESS OF NARCISSISTS

Narcissist has chronic emptiness--the pain of being an empty shell. Despite their identities, it's hell.

The PAIN of the chronic reality that "nothing is real" or the "self is a fiction". So they run to get some.

FALLEN CHURCHES

When you say to the narcissist: how could you change so fast? It's because he has no identity/is miscast.

They want an identity when they have none, they wanna be a beautiful painting on a blank canvas son.

They make up gimmicks for their identity. Stuff they do, wear, their past-times but it's not true reality.

What gave me identity was getting wood for the stove, cat box clean, dogs fed, early nights, studies read.

As basic as it can be, the most essential--the quintessential--gave me **IDENTITY** that's all.

God had to strip me down to the **MOST** essential--wood for the fire, etc.--to find my identity /go higher.

DRAMA IS TOO COSTLY

They'll build you up in order to let you down. We live in a narcissist society and in truth it's all around.

Narcs love drama and seeing you in pain over it. When things are stable they can't resist causing it.

They wanna see you horrified, sad, apprehensive, seen as bad--and they'll do anything to accomplish that.

There's a "tug" when they wanna pull you into drama. Don't take the bait, lock the gate momma.

Therapy: **DETACH** from drama they're trying to create. Note it, separate, walk away gently mate.

The most invasive is when they come into your home and impose drama/expectations/accusations.

With drama we don't meddle in it. We don't talk back. With drama we transcend to stay high: fact.

FALLEN CHURCHES

It's not merely not-beneficial to your well-being, it sucks the life right outa ya so you cannot succeed.

They cause you to waste energy on things not beneficial and to get off your path and life's purpose!

This drama causes you to fall out of your peaceful experience of life: A balmy breeze/lovely night.

Drama is costly. Resolving things with the least drama is the way you wanna go.

It's too much emotional energy to waste on drama when it is unnecessary. Some love it but won't succeed.

I always stop and ask: Am I being pulled into unnecessary drama right now? Pull back into the elements: wow!

No contact: Out of the drama field, out of the snake pit, not reacting, re-attending to things mattering to me.

LIFE IS A PIE: DON'T WASTE ENERGY

Life's a pie and we have limited energy. Why spend it on drama when it's just the spin off of weaklings?

No Contact: NOT engaging, NOT reacting but becoming Stone Faced. That's the result of hurting the Ace.

Ask yourself: is this a life or death situation or the end of the world? Or just someone causing trouble?

Codependency is also known as "pathological loneliness" while dominated and trapped in mind games.

"Bootcamp" was allowing others to determine my reality, to deflect from the lonely pain inside of me.

To wall off feelings from a broken heart we seek outer distractions: a new relationship, a phone, a car.

HOW TO BE A DIVINE WRITER

God does miracles--marvelous works and wonders--and He uses people. He's using me, it's incredible.

If you write, let it be divine: DON'T WRITE unless it first comes through your mind: that's refined.

Don't make stuff up or try to be cute. Let it COME THRU then perfect the sentence--that's good fruit.

Don't write/say things you think they wanna hear, or to gain their approval/avoid disapproval--that's a bore.

Always have pad and pen ready for when it COMES THRU. These are the gems so success will accrue.

Don't say puerile, silly or obvious things you think are true--for great genius comes in brutal reversals.

To all writers: If it doesn't come THROUGH you don't write just cuz you think you should! It's dry as wood.

Genius resolves contradiction in TERSE words and brutal logic reversals that bring insight to real truth.

We all have something we do best/better than others. Maybe you're misdirected and it's not too clever.

Maybe you're forcing creativity and it just sounds silly. Don't do this--be clever, not so obvious.

Don't say/write what you THINK you're supposed to say. This comes off most stilted and boring, ok?

Don't say things to get their approval/avoid disapproval. This is the worst/most puerile: rotten tomatoes.

FALLEN CHURCHES

What we need to do is not wall off/distract but get INTO IT [brokenness] now that we know the process.

Addictions are a deflection from the heart pain which is why they're so obdurate (self-reinforcing).

Can't stop eating because the bio-sensual is the most common distraction from the inner heart call.

Food for women, sex for men: it's all a distraction from the inner pain of having your heart broken again.

I stopped this process thru SOLITUDE, facing self without distraction, drilling deep into the early rejection.

I felt the pain--so my mother didn't like me, so what?--and got into the moment: the elements like rain.

My mother didn't like me cuz I wouldn't conform to her reality. I was artistic and saw God differently.

I was also a stranger to my sisters who had introjected the liberal narrative totally. They ganged up those 3.

When I found/loved the rejected child inside my mal-adaptative addictions instantly subsided.

FORGIVE PEOPLE, LOVE ELEMENTS

I forgave mom and fell in love with the sound of rain on a tin roof, a balmy afternoon, vastness and solitude.

I forgave my betraying unfaithful sisters and switched to God, angels, elements and WORDS of the Master.

Living under others' control--codependency--is a dark place and unhappy rollercoaster life, believe me.

The more dark/depressed my reality the more I held onto people who were bad for me, with tenacity.

FALLEN CHURCHES

Relieved stability [whew]: can't believe I experienced these things, proving how fast life can turn on you.

Having older sister troubles I gravitated to elder feminists and my life became miserable/unstable.

Until we drill deep and work it out, we're forever attracting CORRECTIONS for the original trauma.

We seek distractions from hurt for a feeling of fulfillment which never comes, so we seek for more fun.

The fear of abandonment is actually fear of lost distraction--the bandaid on our heart pain hon'.

It's a wake-up call that our replacement reality--of bandaids--doesn't work [healthy shock].

Replacement reality or independently feeling joy in life and FREEDOM? Complete isolation did it for me hon'

The more we avoid heart pain thru plastic realities the worst the pain gets believe me.

I only began to feel freedom/joy of the independent Self when I went to the root of my pain and solved it.

EXHAUSTION FROM CODEPENDENCY

When out of this exhausting system of seeking distractions for pain, we feel joy--the default setting.

Chicken or the egg? First her sisters hated/rejected her then she became a raving maniac seeking cure.

Now there will be no obstructions to what is ours naturally--the joy of being alive, the true self of mind.

Without these people obstructions and crutches, joy and success are just natural consequences.

FALLEN CHURCHES

Is joy/abundance natural dear, or is it working hard against our will in the wrong direction out of fear?

The only reason we don't have this abundant life is living in our distractions in fear of what's inside.

Liberal trendies are licking toilet seats to spread the coronavirus disease and kill the boomers.

Virus is siege--psychological warfare--with a kernel of truth at the center but a giant grab of POWER.

Ok, massive addictions are a distraction from massive rejection--but you still gotta root it out son.

The churches should have saved us from all this but since they've been fallen it's a wide open ditch.

WITLESS WOMEN

Her life revolves around socializing, yours around work--so what do you have in common with that jerk?

She's a virtue-signaling liberal, a traitor to her race. She puts them up/you down cuz you gotta white face.

I forgive my mother for chiming in with my sisters against me, all to get approval of the female community.

They don't know what they're talking about, just agreeing with each other like a flock of birds flying together.

They'll switch just as suddenly as the flight pattern of the flock changes and you can't pin em down either.

The feminist movement: the worst of the hens got together and decided they were better than men.

Many didn't get the love they needed so became world famous stars instead, it sort of freed em.

FALLEN CHURCHES

All those years I adapted to liberalism without knowing why I felt so sad, sick, depressed, in the dumps.

When in doubt, put it in the "maybe" folder then throw out the "maybe" folder--now have perfect order.

Tho' all works out perfectly your childhood schema says it'll blow apart and you'll have nothing, ok?

EVIL IS AN ENDLESS RABBIT HOLE

The most wonderful and productive president America's ever had. Only an idiot would see him as bad.

The world is going to hell because people no longer use common sense in favor of their "intellect".

Evil is a bottomless pit: there is no end to it as it gets more perverse as we--even we--accept it.

No Hitler or Hussein shows the ends of evil, it is endless as it gets more sick, caricatured by weird people.

Get involved with evil or its people and you're carried downstream in a riptide/mad max dose-dive.

Get involved with evil, can't leave when you want--it costs more/causes more trouble than you ever thought.

Adultery can be physical or mental/emotional. When you think about em too much you're in trouble.

Drama is costly but when it's virtual you have the added problem of a plastic reality--shun it baby.

We're either humble or someone who's about to be humbled.

Most insult comes from extreme jealousy. The communist spirit prevails and they wanna control what you say.

FALLEN CHURCHES

What kept us from success? Outer distractions to avoid inner pain--we woulda had it with constraint.

"I wanna be alone/don't want anyone around" woulda settled it but I was too weak to defend home.

All you do is think about him/her: failure. All you do is think about Him: God--whatever you do prospers.

LOVE ADDICTION

Love addiction is the most obdurate of all, even heroin. Don't allow it to take over, pray to your Father.

I have learned my lesson from all you put me through and won't lessen it by incessant thoughts of you.

A child chooses the shiny bow but God says be patient and think long term, you'll have far more.

There is no more societal restraint. Even women are pugnacious/will wreck the rep of female saints.

The minute I got into town the women took me on. The got together, sized me up and brought me down.

The more kissy-huggy women get the more treacherous they are in fact--watch how they treat dissidents.

Don't talk about your age--don't give in to prevalent ageism! It's irrelevant, you're just a person.

It's not the men I feared, but the women. I'll never forget being raked over the coals/having my rep ruined.

She wrecked your rep to your family, your children, your extended family/friends. No small thing man.

Wrecking a rep is called CALUMNY--soul murder. God will repay her endless gossiping/slander for sure.

FALLEN CHURCHES

GOSSIP-called-"concern" is the weapon of women during their virtue-signaling and it's really mean man.

And yet everyone--lay and professionals alike--see women as victims though they're in control.

CALUMNY IS SOUL MURDER

There's more calumny/soul murder in families than anywhere else--they'll tell strangers about the louse.

With the silent calumny you feel triggered but can't put your finger on it--it's everything above darnit.

Triggered by the invisible disaster you may abuse alcohol rather than confront the calumny in that bad girl.

Sisters hurt me so much it's seared into my nervous system: the devices used to keep us DOWN.

All this comes from fallen churches. When no one knows what true character is they fall to evil devices.

Even if they fail to find a flaw they'll pull the age card. There is no winning with the low, go higher.

Stop talking about your age. That's identity politics--get off of it. You're a person, an artist, an intellect.

When a society loses restraint, lines and decency all hell breaks loose on our psychologies.

Bad associations cause us to make wrong decisions then decades are lost to confusion/destruction.

All I know is he solves problems and keeps my head above water. A stable home is essential for a writer.

Back then when I was an idiot I allowed you in to cause confusion/rain on my parade/bash my plans.

FALLEN CHURCHES

But now as a mature adult with boundaries I am joyfully protected against intrusion by you wanna-bes.

I think you and I could make it together if we could just get past the persecutions of the officious/unclever.

Whenever thoughts of foes arise I substitute with extreme gratitude that I'm totally protected now and wise.

DON'T LET EM HURT YOU TWICE

Don't let him hurt you twice: First by his presence and now by more thoughts of that thief in the night.

Cruel, cruel, cruel. Women are cruel cuz they don't have centuries to temper power, while feeling so cool.

Without his Dad he has just his mother, a fool boasting of feminist power without wisdom to back her.

Don't talk about your age--that's irrelevant--but DO talk about ageism which is PREVALENT.

I came from a sheltered home but they didn't teach me how to maintain privacy/keep out the leaven.

I had to LEARN to draw lines after being with swine and it took a long time to see psychological crimes.

It's not that you're having problems turning 60 but you're encountering cruel ageism remarks, see?

Both racism/ageism comes from good and evil--otherwise they don't exist. Confront em when you see this.

The youth have no more respect for elders. They'll call you "pussy" and other trivializing degraders.

You must insist on elder respect like traditional cultures who adore their old. When they attack be bold.

FALLEN CHURCHES

I fear change and desire to sit on the fence.

What do you suppose could satisfy the soul but to walk free and know no superior? Walt Wiltman

Inability to get over rejectors indicates inner wounds needing healing, or you wouldn't want em.

Remove the person--it isn't "him" or "her" it's the gaping inner wound of broken bonds from years prior.

Even those people weren't important but their rejection occurred early before you realized about em.

EMOTIONALLY BLOCKED FROM EARLY TRAUMA

Blocked emotionally at the early trauma, you're a baby viewing the world as mean/dark like momma.

Feminists are witches and their devices to control us bring the stain of illogic deep in the minds of all of us.

They don't view the world logically for that would seem unfair, see? It's all what they want it to be.

Having a broken trauma bond with a witch leaves a stain on consciousness: resentment, anxiousness.

It matters not that your persecutors are dead. The imprint remains in how you see the world or dread it.

Going after someone who's rejected you is a **NATURAL RESPONSE** of someone who's been wounded.

Yearning for a rejector indicates an inner wound that is **CRYING OUT** for attention--it's not about him.

Going after a rejector feels like the right thing to do when under delusive **REPETITION COMPULSIONS.**

FALLEN CHURCHES

The rejector seems dashing--the shiny object--when usually he's an Elmer Fudd, a dud, not much.

Carrying a torch for years is that gaping inner wound that never healed over silly, stupid, obsolete people.

But the baby didn't know that so here you are: an aging baby still hung up on an early trauma/tragedy.

We're trying to become whole thru this other person--present relationships are just past patterns.

The answer is to hold and love yourself as if you're that baby. Relive the early tragedy, feel it, cry.

Running after a rejector indicates internal trauma that's not just unhealed but abscessing every moment.

It's your job to take control and be compassionate to self. You're responsible for you so you must.

ARTISTICALLY EXPRESSING HURT

The needed self-compassion comes out thru ART: drawing, journals even self-design has a part.

Artistically expressing our hurt feelings: what are we doing, what are we feeling, what is going on?

For years I heard women yelling at me inside. Mean, nasty, ruthless "introjections"--a gaping hole undefined.

You wanna run after your loving/devoted mom and dad not a ruthless user who discarded you and left.

Where there is mental illness or alcoholism in the mother there will be trauma in son/daughter forever.

You were IMPRINTED like a baby duck following it's rejecting, ugly, angry mother covered in mud.

FALLEN CHURCHES

That's when we make em into Gods: dashing important people we lost, adored cuz we saw em as boss.

It's self love to catch yourself in the act rather than running after people who couldn't care less.

See yourself running to your art or study not to alcohol, distractions or love addictions to persons.

When I got into solitude/study my inner reality exploded. I knew who I was: values genetically encoded.

WORSHIP IS FORTIFICATION

Worship fortified me. I began to feel whole not scattered, putting up boundaries was all that mattered.

To heal you must be heard, seen and understood. That's why counsel is important, not trying to be "good".

When I finally found someone I could talk to--my husband--my reality healed/someone understood.

Realizing that evil wickedness is the default setting for humans is a milestone--a shock that heals son.

Sisters told me people are good--are you kidding me? So disparate from my own reality, God help me.

I could see thru em but they couldn't and just that put me in the untouchable, hated, scapegoated class.

If you don't accept the plastic reality that fakers are "good", you're a foe, hated and misunderstood.

How I quieted those thoughts: walking in the sun, playing with cats and dogs, lovely music and travel logs.

I saw at death all these bad memories would dissolve like vapors, a mere bleep in eternity, gone forever.

FALLEN CHURCHES

I saw her as the meanest/most snooty witch ever but she was the angel in their hearts, beloved forever.

How could I allow these know-nothing nobodies to ruin and determine MY reality all these dark days?

When you are longing for someone who has rejected/hurt you that's your OWN wound crying to be heard.

Gaping inner wounds trigger immune responses/bloody schemas that never work, just more trauma.

Anyone with open inner wounds is walking trouble cuz it's never about the beautiful now just a guy she knows.

The town slut was molested as a child then via her flying monkeys she attacked everyone around.

THE CHILD NEEDS YOUR ATTENTION

The inner baby is crying out but doesn't need THEIR attention just YOUR attention--catch it hon'.

Modern miracle: we can find youtube mentors who speak to our child's broken heart/give us a fresh start.

Youtube mentors--Jenna & Trevor--tied loose ends together/I had results when ties were severed.

The study of trauma bonds showed me my whole life when doomed. Boom, boom, boom = integration.

If you think I'm gonna get involved with you after enduring the petty/cruel you're a dam fool.

Once trauma bonds are cleaned up/healed over you vet all associates as the most important thing ever.

Trying for independence while remaining enmeshed: Now here's a mess: flying monkeys and all the rest.

FALLEN CHURCHES

Past actors are gone--YOU are the only one capable of full-filling that hole, a power you had all along.

To be there for yourself, using various methods like worship, prayer, meditation, nature, study.

Videos helped me immeasurably. Reason, light, love, non-shaming, acceptance and understanding.

Jenna and Trevor my youtube mentors ran it down to me and all at once I knew the enemy/saw eternity.

People are cruel. They'll use you until they don't need you then discard you AND stab you in the back too.

You love yourself by cutting off people who are toxic: walking away, setting boundaries/being firm about it.

CURE: CREATE A SPACE FOR SELF

By creating a space for SELF that is your own [tiny cabin], by going out in nature. Find SELF = for sure.

Promiscuous female [who'd been imposed on] busted boundaries constantly, that's how it repeats honey.

Their just reward is their own dark, empty, toothless future cuz God is angry every day at those lechers.

Thinking I had to adapt to them I'd get into crying sessions. My reality was the demons in em.

Her flying monkeys were her Johns and they'd do anything to keep sex addiction to that broad.

Years of darkened reality from fallen friends/family is more layers to remove, revealing heaven = orderly.

You're healing correctly by taking long walks, sun bathing and exercising--to be God's peculiar darling.

FALLEN CHURCHES

It all comes down to unmet needs and toxic shame. Focus in and study the system from which you came.

Every time you want to be approved of as **OK** by an external source you're running from your Self.

It's actually you that needs you and you've got to be there for yourself. With time/music it all works out.

I didn't know my family until I started to escape. That's when the devil came out in real heartbreak.

I can hear women yelling at me--these are inner voices of our **INTROJECTIONS**: people incorporated in.

HELLO, GOODBYE

I can't say goodbye if I never said hello. A flash in the pan I guess or a test from below? I'm still glad to know.

I guess you reminded me of someone or they reminded me of you. It's an eternal thing, maybe love too.

When we die we have no memory of this earth. All things vaporize into nothing tho' we were so serious.

All that stress from human duress stripped me of all immunity and lost logic to the [loose] flesh.

The constant triangulations, the evil gossip and the flying monkey attacks made her an erratic lunatic.

By creating space for **SELF** that is your own [tiny cabin] or going out in nature you'll find your Self for sure.

How quickly all things disappear. Marcus Aurelius

Women are **MEAN**. It's not them it's a spirit that's made a home in them, they're now on top they said.

FALLEN CHURCHES

Indoor cats: 13-17 years. Outdoor cats: 2-5 years. You choose but indoor cats are happier/healthier.

Bioweapons are not new. We gave wool blankets filled with small pox to kill ALL the Indians too.

Events were so traumatic I went into denial just to get thru them. Later when safe PTSD made me view em.

They tortured you to see how much you could take. It's a play by little men for petty power's sake.

The narcissist always has someone else do his dirty work. His hands are clean/flying monkeys do the curse.

Her hands were always clean while her cohorts would hate and come after me: now I see the scene.

HURT TWICE, NO DICE

Lovebombing triggers fantasy hormones and traumatic bonds thru intermittent reinforcement.

Intermittent reinforcement, pulling back, blowing hot and cold and mixed signals keep you hooked.

I will NOT let you hurt me twice. First by your presence and second by my angry resentments.

First he stung me like a pit viper, then his venomous influence hung on in memories of the torture.

And yet when I saw him again he was a weaselly loser cuz God breaks the teeth of all wicked mockers.

He would smile sweetly meanwhile his monkeys would steal from me then it was all my fault you see.

Part of PTSD is assuming things will go wrong. You're hypervigilant and leery, you don't belong.

FALLEN CHURCHES

But that was under a curse when God was angry at you every day until repentance--now you're ok.

The police state is enforced by petty cogs in the wheel who LOVE being mean forcing shifting rules.

The coronavirus tester LOVED shoving that stick up your nose and grinding it in--that's a shit test son.

What is the enveloping fear of the police state? It's dread of petty bureaucrats and little thugs who hate.

Because there's two different camps: those who want a pro-human expansion and a post-human one.

Repentant Christians shall NOT be condemned--it's ERASED thru Jesus, God no remember it.

Repentant sin is as far away as East from West at the deepest part of the ocean--now don't go fishin'

Gotta KNOW God erased it/buried it cuz His Son was the atonement and without any doubt that covers it.

They hate you when you don't conform to their expectations and just that's too much ma'am.

FOR HEALTH REASONS

Fruits and vegetables: De-age, no bloat--that's what it's all about. They are alkaline, the rest is not.

There are only the best, no "maybes". if it's a maybe you should throw it in the trash baby.

My sleeping has become cat-naps whenever I crash. There is no time to waste, it's success or bust.

I may not feel like eating a raisin, date or fig--but I like healthy candies, it's the combo that tastes great.

FALLEN CHURCHES

Afternoons are fasting, movies without sound [North by Northwest, 1959] with view/music in the background.

Beautiful movies and sets with clever scripts and gorgeous people but no plot cuz it's music you got.

North by Northwest [1959] was right before things changed for good. Class, elegance, manhood.

I need music to re-organize my mind. The world is too confusing, interruptions abound, I seek refined.

Just music and great movies without sound and fantastic views while dreaming of eternity and You.

Sex is too easy man. What makes you better than dogs, goats, pigs, even cockroaches to it. Don't say it.

KAREN'S HEALTHY CANDIES

Karen's Healthy Candies: Coconut, nuts, figs, dates, raisins, honey, nutbutter, cacao, cacao/coco butter.

Filled with carbs and I don't care--it's superfoods and incredibly detoxifying as grandma knew before.

Karen's Kandies, mango-coconut smoothie, piece cheese, few nuts. Bloated from an avo-alergy so that's out.

Watch hybrids like "smokehouse almonds"--tho' delicious they're cut with crap: you will bloat/throw em out.

Mango smoothies, Karen's Healthy Candies, cheese or buttered corn [a fruit], homemade pizza.

No more fruits and veggies filled with fecal sludge from the cities--they aren't working for me anymore, truly.

Smokehouse almonds are mostly fake--filled with soy, corn starch and other things we should hate!

FALLEN CHURCHES

ALMONDS? Or are they veg oil, corn maltodextrin, yeast, hydrolyzed corn and soy protein--come on!

Karen's Healthy Candies [KHC] has the highest acid-binding properties ala Arnold Ehret.

Raisins bind mucus at a rate of 12, figs 30, dates 14, and then nuts, coconut, cacao and cocao/coco butter.

It's the synergy of all these "dessert fruits" taken together that is most powerful/slimming and delicious.

My healthy candy today is predominantly fig in that mix, the highest mucus-eliminator given a 30.

FORGET NIGHTSHADES, THINK STORAGE

Gave my nightshades to the rabbits: tomatoes, bells, potatoes. Lettuce too, sludge from city ghettos.

Frozen mango for the smoothie with bottled coco cream, nut butters and your candy. Morning dandy.

Then have some homemade pizza with good dough and lotsa cheese on top. For the whole day, that's all.

If you wanna cheat in the aft, have a piece of candy. You already know it's superior tho' also delicious.

Dry mix: blend nuts, coco flakes, raisins, dates, figs. Melt and spread: cacao, nutbutter, honey, cacao butter.

In other words, I care more about dissolving mucus and acid--the basis of disease--then adding protein.

Figs dissolve acid/mucus at a 30, raisins at a 12--and grape or other juicy only gets a 9. It's the black fruit.

My food storage based on above: frozen mango, corn, mozzarella, canned pineapple and BUTTER.

Healthy candy storage: nutbutters, nuts, coconut flakes/cream, honey, dried fruit, cacao bars/butter.

Store enough for a year of these essential items if following this theory. Buy two more chest freezers.

If you're so sensitive that FRUIT/FAT/FASTING is all that works, you also need the BEST air/water filters.

I bought Alexapure air/water filters from Alex Jones. His whole thing is protection from what's coming folks.

Don't bother with nightshades like you used to, salad crap: tomatoes, bells, potatoes--get stuff to store.

Clothes: cashmere for winter [400x warmer] and rayon or cotton for summer: no synthetics whatsoever!

You can't trust wool companies anymore like Icebreaker--they're lacing their stuff with nylon, use Ebay.

FOOD STORAGE FOR THIS THEORY

Get dough balls for the freezer--boxes of 96. Get caputo dough without soy which most pizzas are made of.

After melting the cement [nutbutters, honey, cacao, cacao/coco butter], spread out with dry mix.

Now put the cookie sheet in freezer. After four hours, break into parts like any brittle, bag up, store.

Use the "brownie brittle" for afternoon snacks if you must and put em in your mango smoothie, it's delicious.

Your animal fats will be cheese and butter. If you like eggs, get a connection for your storage.

For more storage in basement, buy starches: noodles, pasta, rice. Your dough balls go into freeze.

FALLEN CHURCHES

The most famous/beautiful supermodel in the world said: "I go right for the pies, ice cream and cakes".

LONG HAIR

Why must a woman be constantly seen brushing the hair from her eyes? Why not just cut it/come alive?

In the "rare interview" she brushed the hair from her eyes 27 times and I didn't see her as rare/a prize.

Just to have "long hair" you see frizzy, dry, uncontrollable, time-consuming hairstyles everywhere.

The shorter it is the better it looks. It's the "Obama Cut": once a week with 1/8" clipper: sharp!

The professional independent woman pushed the hair from her eyes 30 times in the interview, hah!

Even though I hated him I recommend the Obama Cut for women. 1/8" all over shows head-shape, splendid.

Everyone's got a gimmick--doesn't mean they're not legit. If it'll get you to eat/live healthy, it's worth it.

The trillion dollar bailout is just massive theft packaged as a gift. Mike Adams

CORONAVIRUS AND 5G

DON'T ABANDON PETS. The coronavirus transmission is human to human, not animal to human.

5G is headaches, dizziness and wanna die feeling. Get away then we're ok but can't escape this thing.

We. could opt out of the smart meters [dizziness, headaches] but not the 5G: this is serious!

5G isn't just for faster internet it's to TRACK us and make us sick as we're more easily dominated.

WITHOUT GOD THE SYSTEM IS A DRUG

Had you stayed in nature all woulda been ok but in human systems there was a high price to pay.

The systems trigger old templates and then insane [lunatic] reactions and attempts to escape.

The system acts as a **DRUG** and we all know drugs create insane behavior as brain chemicals are triggers.

The victim of the system has no idea why he acted that way/went into a rage all day in a blackout, ok?

You see this mazeway on family day when the system triggers wild, erratic, "unexplained" insanity.

100 KAREN KELLOCK BOOKS

AFFINITY OR MISERY
AGELESS CORNUCOPIA
AMERICA AWAKE!
AMERICA'S DAFT ERA
ARTS OF PALEO FASTING
AUTOPHAGY ON CHEATERS
BACKSTABBING NEUROTICS
BETRAYAL TRAUMA
BOOMERS AND BROKENNESS
BOOT ON NECK
CHAMPION GUIDES
COMMIE NUTHOUSE
COMMIES
COMMUNIST SPIRIT
CONTAGION OF MADNESS
CONTAGIOUS MADNESS
CULTURE CLASH BASHED
DAFT LEFT
DAILY FASTARIAN
DAM RATS
DIVERSITY IS CRUELTY
E-RACE WHITE
EVIL FREAKS (Beyond Gross)
THE END OR A BEND?
FEMALE BULLIES AND FEMI-NAZIS
FEMALE CARNALITY
FEMALE DUMB DOWN
FEMALE POWER DRIVE
FEMINISM AND RUIN 1 & 2
FIX FOR MISFITS
FOOLS & TRAMPS
FREEDOM SPEAKING
FRENEMY ENABLER
FRENEMY LIAR
FRENEMY THIEF
FRENEMY TRAITOR
TRENEMY TYRANT
GENIUS IS HELD DOWN
GLOBALISLAM
GOD USES THE FLAWED
HAZE OF THE LATTER DAYS

THE HERD IN WORDS
HIX POLITIX
HOW THEY RUINED US
JUST SKIP DINNER
LE FEMME AND THE COMMUNIST SPIRIT
LIBERAL CHAOS & ROT
LIBERAL DOUBLETHINK
LIBERAL GALL 1 & 2
LIBERAL SHOVE-DOWNS
LOCK YOUR GATE
LOSERS and Femme Fatales
MANUAL FOR SUPERIOR MEN
MODERN ART FROM HELL
MOSTLY FAKE
NOTES TO CHAMPS 1 & 2
OVERCOME FRENEMIES
PC MAKES US CRAZY
PEOPLE ARE CRUEL
PEOPLE PROBLEMS 1 & 2
PERSECUTED GENIUIS
POLI-PSYCH MYSTERIES
PRETENTIOUS SLOBS
QUEEN BEE
RED NEW DEAL
RETURNING TO FIRST NATURE
SEASON OF TREASON
SEPARATE MEANS HOLY
SOCIAL HYPNOTISM
SOLITUDE SOLUTION
SUPERCILIOUS
THE SCHOOLS SCREWED EM UP
TOAD TO PRINCE
TRIALS CYCLES
TRUMP VS. GROUP
TRUST IN TRASH
THE TRUTH ABOUT PEOPLE
UNDERHEANDEDLY CLEVER
WALK TALL WITHIN WALLS
WE'RE NOT ALL ONE
WINNERS SKIP DINNER
WORK OR SMERK

AUTHOR BIO

Karen Kellock Ph.D.

Ph.D Political Psychology, UCI 1976
Post-Doctoral: UCI Medical School
Department of Psychiatry
Grants NIMH, NIAAA

Ph.D. dissertation "A Systems-Theoretic View of Pathologic Interaction" made an early mark as the "Wife of the Alcoholic Syndrome". Postdoctoral research at UCI Medical, Dept. of Psychiatry on the systems surrounding pathology on NIMH and NIAAA federal grants: The Contagion of Madness: The Psychology of Neurotic Interaction and Pathological Systems. Therapy tool Therapeutic Playwriting introduced the play Mary and Murv: Gruesome Twosomes in the Alcoholic Marriage. She taught Abnormal Psychology and Pathological Systems Theory at UC and CSU campuses and developed "the Debris Theory of Disease" in 100 books and website: (www.karenkellock.org).

www.ingramcontent.com/pod-product-compliance
Lightning Source LLC
Chambersburg PA
CBHW061721250726

48657CB00002B/714